Traditional
WOODEN
DUMMY

Traditional
WOODEN DUMMY

Ip Man's Wing Chun System

Samuel Kwok & Tony Massengill

EMPIRE Books

P.O. Box 491788, Los Angeles, CA 90049

www.empirebooks.net

First published in 2010 by Empire Books

First edition
10 09 08 07 06 05 04 03 02 01 00

Printed in the United States of America.
Empire Books
P.O. Box 491788
Los Angeles, CA 90049
www.empirebooks.net

ISBN-13: 978-1-933901-46-6
ISBN-10: 1-933901-46-6

Library of Congress Cataloging-in-Publication Data

Kwok, Samuel.
  Wing chun traditional wooden dummy / by Samuel Kwok with Tony Massengill.
-- First American ed.
      p. cm.
  ISBN 978-1-933901-46-6 (pbk. : alk. paper)
  1. Kung fu. I. Massengill, Tony. II. Title.
  GV1114.7.K853 2010
  796.815'9--dc22
                            2010014914

Dedication

This book is dedicated to the late Grandmaster Ip Man who spent his life promoting the Wing Chun Kung Fu system.

Foreword

The Wooden Dummy of the Ip Man system is an invaluable tool for developing technique, structure, power and understanding of Wing Chun.

There are many different variations of the Wooden Dummy set taught throughout the world. The method in this book is the result of studying the original 8MM footage Ip Man filmed just day's prior to his death from throat cancer in December 1972, along with many years of training and research with many of Ip Man's direct students, including his own sons, Ip Chun and Ip Ching.

It is the hope of the authors that this book can be of some assistance to those wanting to gain a more full understanding of the Ip Man Wing Chun system.

~ Samuel Kwok and Tony Massengill

Acknowledgements

I'd like to express my sincerest thanks to all those who have made the creation of this book possible.

My wife Xin Lou Kwok, my son Jason and daughter Annie, and my stepson Dong Ni. I need to thank my parents Rev. Henry Kwok and Mrs. Annie Wai Chun Kwok, my brothers and sisters especially my brother John for their support.

I have been very fortunate in having the opportunity to train under both sons of the late Grandmaster Ip Man. Grandmasters Ip Chun and Ip Ching, both great Kung Fu men, and genuine gentlemen.

It is thanks to their generous attitudes and personalities that I was given unique access to the knowledge passed to them through their father. Grandmaster Ip Man was fortunate in having access to the knowledge and skills developed by two Masters, Chan Wah Shun and Leung Bik. He was able to glean great insight into the differences in application due to the very different physical stature of these two Masters.

I have also benefited from the knowledge and experience of other Ip Man students, such as Wong Shun Leung, Tsiu Sheng Tin, Chan Wai Hong, Lok Yiu and Lee Sing. I also owe these men a debt of gratitude.

I'd like to say a special thanks to my disciple Tony Massengill for his work in co-authoring this book. I also thank Stephen Rigby for his help in the photos, all my instructors around the world who continue to spread and preserve the traditional Ip Man Wing Chun system. Then last, but by no means least may I thank all my loyal students whose determination to learn, honor and preserve this traditional Chinese martial art is wonderful to see.

Samuel Kwok

The development of this book has been a labor of love for me. The Wooden Dummy is a great training tool, not only for Wing Chun, but one which can be utilized by all martial artist to develop a more thorough understanding of their skills. Anytime one undertakes a project such as this there are many people to thank. First of all I need to thank my Lord and savior, Jesus Christ, for the blessings he has allowed me to experience. I want to thank my beautiful wife Yongnan for her patience and understanding when I spent many long hours pecking on the keys of my computer, taking time away from her.

I need to thank my students Lafayette Harris and Jeff Benton for helping run my school in the times I had to be away to work on this book, as well as Tim Phillips and Chris Gibbs for building the portable frame for the Dummy used in the photos. Also to Jay (DAZ) McCollum for proofreading the manuscript.

I need to thank my mentor and big brother, Glen Moore, for his guidance and advice and friendship throughout my years of training.

And finally my Sigungs Ip Chun and Ip Ching and my Sifu, Samuel Kwok for the treasure he has passed to me.

Tony Massengill

木人樁

7

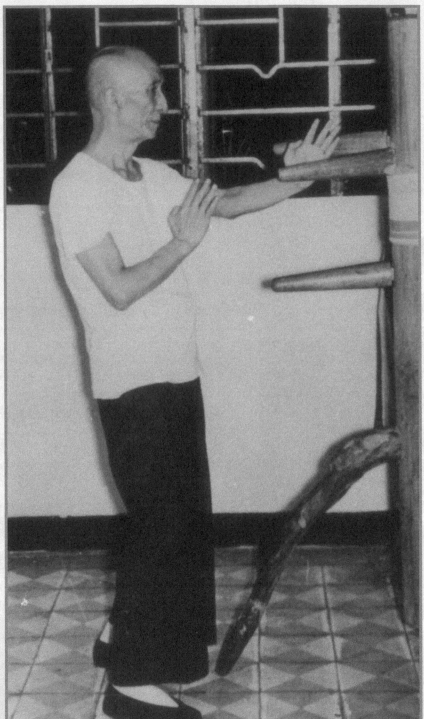

CONTENTS

木人椿

About the Authors

Grandmaster Samuel Kwok

Samuel Kwok is a 2nd Generation Master of Wing Chun Kung Fu under the tradition passed through the Ip Man Family. He was born in Hong Kong in 1948, the son of a Church Minister. He became interested in the martial arts at an early age. His formal introduction to the Martial Arts was in the White Crane Kung Fu system, under the guidance of his uncle Luk Chi Fu. His Wing Chun training began in 1967 under Chan Wai Ling in Hong Kong.

In 1972 Samuel Kwok moved from Hong Kong to the United Kingdom to study and pursue a career in psychiatric nursing. While living in London, he went to the Church of Reverend Kao who was a good friend of this father. Reverend Kao told him about one of the members of the congregation, who was a Wing Chun teacher named Lee Sing. Lee Sing was a student of Sifu Lok Yiu and Chiu Wan. Before Lee Sing left Hong Kong he became a student of Ip Man. Furthermore while in Hong Kong, Lee Sing also learnt Leng Jan style Wing Chun. After meeting Lee Sing, Samuel Kwok became his student in 1973.

Samuel Kwok began teaching in 1975. He started by teaching his friends and fellow student nurses from the hospital but later went onto teaching the general public. Samuel Kwok was confused by the fact that everyone's Wing Chun forms were different and so in 1978 he returned to Hong Kong in the hope of finding the true source of Wing Chun. Samuel Kwok was introduced by Lee Sing to Grandmaster Ip Man's eldest son, Grandmaster Ip Chun. It was later, during their second meeting that Ip Chun offered to teach Samuel Kwok the Wooden Dummy techniques. Samuel Kwok realized that he was being given a great honor so he accepted. At this time, Ip Chun was only teaching part time.

For the next few years Samuel Kwok had private tuition from Ip Chun and after gaining Master level in Wing Chun, he opened his first school in Hong Kong and it was not long before his students began making a name for themselves at tournaments and demonstrations in the colony.

Before returning to the UK Master Kwok made a vow to Ip Chun that he would promote his master and Wing Chun throughout the world. Upon returning to the

UK, in 1981 he was appointed as the chairman and senior overseas representative of the *Ip Chun Martial Art Association* by Grandmaster Ip Chun.

After settling in the UK, Master Kwok began to teach Wing Chun privately. Later he opened his first school because of the great demand for his instruction. After settling in the UK Master Kwok started teaching first in St.Annes-on-sea and then in Manchester and later throughout the country. In 1985 in his effort to promote Traditional Wing Chun and his Si-Fu, Master Kwok held the first of many seminars in the UK for Grandmaster Ip Chun.

In 1986 Master Kwok's first book "The Path to Wing Chun" was published and has sold copies all over the world. It has helped beginners and martial artists from different styles to understand the art of Wing Chun "Kung Fu". It has been so successful that it is currently in its 6th edition as it has often been reprinted to keep it up to date.

In 1983 The Chinese Society of Lancaster University invited Samuel Kwok to teach Wing Chun to university students. This was a great success and in later years students at the university set up a Lancaster University Wing Chun Club. Master Kwok still teaches at the university club to this day, and the average yearly membership of this club often sores well over 100 members.

In 1992 Master Kwok invited both Grandmasters Ip Chun and Ip Ching to the UK, to hold their first joint seminars across the country; it was during this visit that Kwok was able to begin learning from Grandmaster Ip Ching as well. This was Grandmaster Ip Ching's first visit to the UK.

In 1994 Master Kwok returned to Hong Kong and at the suggestion of Grandmaster Ip Chun, resumed training with his brother, Grandmaster Ip Ching, in order to gain a different perspective on the Wing Chun system. That same year Master Kwok helped to organize some very successful seminars in America, taught by Grandmaster Ip Chun.

In 1995 once again Grandmaster Ip Ching was invited by Master Kwok to the UK, to conducted several seminars across the country but this time he was accompanied by Grandmaster Chu Sheung Tin, one of the first students in Hong Kong of the late Grandmaster Ip Man. Also in 1995 the two famous brothers Grandmaster Ip Chun and Ip Ching were brought to Chicago by Samuel Kwok to teach together for the first time in America.

In 1998 Master Samuel Kwok received a BA honor from Manchester University for his life time achievement and promotion of Martial Arts. Today Master Kwok is constantly promoting Wing Chun across the world by conducting and organizing seminars, competitions, demonstrations, as well as producing books and videos with Empire Media and Empire Books.

In 1999 Samuel Kwok performed demonstrations with his students at the 1st World Ving Tsun Conference that was held in Hong Kong. The success of this led to Samuel Kwok also performing again at the 2nd World Ving Tsun Conference.

Samuel Kwok sees the conferences as a great opportunity to promote Ip Man's Wing Chun in a way that Ip Man would be proud of.

In 2001 Samuel Kwok and many of his students and instructors from around the world once again showed their dedication to Ip Family Wing Chun by traveling to Fat Shan/Foshan in Southern China to help Grandmaster Ip Ching promote the Ip Man Tong. They performed demonstrations to help promote the opening of the museum dedicated to Ip Man. The museum was opened in 2002.

In 2007 Samuel Kwok was honored in Fat Shan/Foshan, China when the book "Mastering Wing Chun – The Keys to Ip Man's Kung Fu" which he co-wrote with his disciple Tony Massengill, was placed in the Ip Man museum.

Master Kwok also runs a yearly training camp in Mallorca, Spain where students and instructors from around the world can come to perfect their skills in the art of Wing Chun. Master Kwok also helps to arrange tours and training in Hong Kong with Grandmasters Ip Chun and Ip Ching, for his students, showing that like himself he wants his students to benefit from this great master first hand.

Master Kwok is the leader of the *Traditional Ip Man Wing Chun Association* with schools around the world. Those interested in more information on Master Samuel Kwok, or information on authorized instructors around the world can visit:

www.ipmanwingchun.com

Grandmaster Samuel Kwok is available for private tuition, seminars and instructor tuition.

For details feel free to contact Grandmaster Kwok directly:

Phone – 07856265889 or – 07753191680

Or email: kwokwingchun@hotmail.com

www.kwokwingchun.com

Sifu Tony Massengill

Tony has been involved in the Martial Arts for over forty years, and has earned Black Belt rank or instructor certification in several disciplines, including Kenpo, Thai Boxing, Chin-Na, Tae Kwon Do and various Stick and Knife systems.

He is retired from a career in public safety where he worked for over twenty-five years serving as a police officer, firefighter and emergency medic. Over the span of his career he developed training programs and taught many in the field of law enforcement, emergency medical services and the military.

Tony began training in the Wing Chun Kung Fu system in 1979. Over the years that have passed he has trained with several instructors, but finally found a home under Master Samuel Kwok. Tony was accepted as a private disciple and was eventually awarded Master level certification by Master Kwok in June 2005.

When asked about his background and his experience under Master Kwok, Tony states "I have been involved in the Martial Arts since the age of five. After training extensively in many fighting methods, I settled on Wing Chun as the system I felt was the best for my goals, which was combat effectiveness in the street, not the ring". But settling on Wing Chun was just the beginning of my journey.

After pursuing Wing Chun under many instructors, several of which were very well known, I had the opportunity to meet and experience Master Kwok's Wing Chun, and immediately knew I had found what I was looking for. I had worked for many years as a public safety professional, so I knew what REAL fights were on the streets, so I am not easily impressed by instructors demonstrating their supposed "Deadly Effectiveness". But with Samuel Kwok's Wing Chun, I was blown away. This feeling was further solidified when I was in Hong Kong and Fat shan/foshan, China with Master Kwok, and saw first hand how much respect everyone there has for this great Kung Fu man".

Tony was selected to be Master Kwok's demonstration partner at the 2nd World Wing Chun Conference held in Hong Kong in 2005. Tony is the senior U.S. Representative of Master Kwok and has been appointed to administer Kwok's association in the United States.

In 2007 Tony Massengill was honored in Fat Shan/Foshan, China when the book "Mastering Wing Chun – The Keys to Ip Man's Kung Fu" which he co-wrote with his Sifu, Grandmaster Samuel Kwok, was placed in the Ip Man museum.

Tony resides in Gloucester, Virginia U.S.A. and teaches Wing Chun full-time at his school **MASS Martial Arts**, in Yorktown, Virginia, the U.S. Headquarters of the **Traditional Ip Man Wing Chun Association**, founded by Grandmaster Kwok.

Those interested in contacting Tony Massengill can visit his school's web site at: **www.massmartialarts.com** or e-mail him at: **sifu@massmartialarts.com**

Or call (757) 846-1188

Introduction

Mook Yan Jong is the Chinese name for the Wooden Dummy and is pronounced "muck-yahn-chong". In Chinese history, the Wooden Dummy is said to originate from the Shaolin monastery of Mt. Sung in the Honan province of China, where it is said that there was a hall or corridor of dummies through which the Shaolin Monks must pass to show the skills that they had at their disposal. These dummies had moveable arms and legs, controlled by the monks, which were used to test the skills of the monks.

In the more recent past, two types of Jong are used in Kung Fu training. These are the Dai Jong placed into the ground and the more modern Gua Jong that is attached to a wall. The modern Gua Jong was devised by Great Grandmaster Ip Man when he moved to Hong Kong and it was necessary to have the Jong situated in an apartment. The first modern Gua Jong was made by Fung Shek for

Great Grandmaster Ip Man and was placed in his school in 1956. In 2002, Great Grandmaster Ip Man's personal Jong was placed in the Ip Man Tong Museum in Fat Shan/Foshan, China.

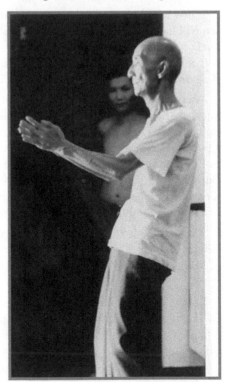

The Jong is a wooden stake that allows the Wing Chun practitioner to hone his or her Kung Fu skills. The Wing Chun version of the Jong has three arms and one leg, which represents an opponent's body in various positions. The Dummy consists of a cylindrical body of approximately five feet in length and nine inches in diameter, with two upper arms at shoulder level, a lower arm at stomach height, and one leg, suspended on a framework by two crosspieces. The Jong has some degree of movement when force is applied due to flex in the horizontal slats that reduces the risk of impact injury through forceful contact and returns some of that force back into the practitioner, testing their stance and arm structure. The Jong's purpose is to reinforce correct structures and angles, to

Photo taken by Ip Chun during the filming of the 8MM. Ip Ching looks on.

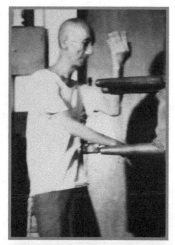

foster the development of flow and to allow the correct, full expression of Fa Jing (last moment energy) which we can never use on a live training partner without the risk of seriously injuring them.

The Jong is an integral part of Wing Chun Kung Fu training as passed by the Ip family. Training in the traditional Jong form is usually initiated after completing the training of the first two empty hand Wing Chun forms. There are however, some instructors who hold the training until after all three empty hand forms have been completed, while others may even introduce sections of the Jong form early in a student's training in order to create structure and understanding of the method being taught.

The Jong is in many ways the perfect home training device. It takes the place of a training partner when training solo. It helps to correct footwork, upper body structure, proper blocking and attacking angles as well as the coordination of all of these factors in one harmonious movement. And, unlike other training devices such as the Western Boxing heavy bag, the Jong lends itself to both offensive and defensive training, where the heavy bag has limited use as a defensive training tool.

While this book is about the Ip Man Wing Chun method of Wooden Dummy training, there are many elements of the Jong which can be adapted in order to enhance the training of other systems as well. Those interested can use the methods presented here as a conceptual foundation to guide them in incorporating Wooden Dummy training into their personal training no matter what system of Martial Arts they follow.

CHAPTER 1

Wing Chun's History

The stories handed down through the generations hold that the Wing Chun system was developed in the famous Siu Lum (Shaolin) Temple. The system was said to have been taught to a young woman named Yim Wing Chun by a Siu Lum nun named Ng Mui. Yim Wing Chun eventually married a martial artist named Leung Bok Cho, to whom she taught the method. Leung Bok Cho in turn taught Leung Lan Kwai, Leung Yee Tai, Wong Wah Bo, and others. Leung Yee Tai and Wong Wah Bo taught Leung Jan, who became a famous fighter and Chinese doctor. Leung Jan taught his son Leung Bik, as well as a merchant named Chan Wah Shun. Ip Man was passed the system first by Chan Wah Shun, and then later in Hong Kong by Leung Bik.

There are many books and articles which debate the history listed above. However with the lack of written records, there is no way of knowing just how accurate this account is. The Wing Chun system as it has been passed down from the late Grandmaster Ip Man up to the present generation, through the teaching of his his students, including his own sons, Grandmasters Ip Chun and Ip Ching is historical fact, so we will concentrate on that segment of Wing Chun's history.

Ip Man was the first to openly teach Wing Chun. He began his teaching career in Foshan, China, and then later in Hong Kong. It is through Ip Man's teaching that Wing Chun has spread throughout the world. Ip Man had many students, but it was Bruce Lee, the famous movie star and "King of Kung Fu" who was the most notable. It

Ip Man with Bruce Lee.

The Ip Family.

was through the fame brought by Bruce Lee that the world became aware of Wing Chun and Lee's teacher, Grandmaster Ip Man. According to the accounts given to Ip Man's sons Ip Chun and Ip Ching (by Ip Man), their father began his training as a young boy. Ip Man (1893-1972) was born at Song Yuen of Foshan, China at the end of the Qing Dynasty. Foshan was situated at the most prosperous region of the Guangdong province. Well known masters of the Southern Kung Fu schools, Wong Fai-hung, Cheung Hungshing, Leung Jan, Leung Siu-ching etc. came from Foshan. Ip Man grew up hearing the stories of the exploits of these great Kung Fu men. So it's not surprising that he would develop into one of the legendary masters himself.

Ip Man's education in Wing Chun began as a youth when he became a student of Chan Wah Shun, who was a student of the famous Leung Jan. Chan Wah Shun rented the Ip family clan hall on the main street of Foshan in order to teach Kung Fu. He accepted Ip Man as a student towards the end of his teaching career when he was quite old. Master Chan was a big man by Chinese standards, so his Kung Fu was powerful. Ip Man learned from Master Chan until the masters' death, and continued his training with his Sihing (Senior) Ng Chun until Ip Man left Foshan for Hong Kong in 1941.

Ip Man moved to Hong Kong at the age of 15 to attend St. Stephens College. There he had a chance meeting with an old gentleman who was a martial artist. This old man crossed hands with Ip Man and beat him soundly. This disturbed Ip Man very much as he had developed his Kung Fu to a high level and considered himself to be quite proficient. As it turned out, the old gentleman was Leung Bik, the son of Ip Man's Sifu, Master Chan Wah Shun's teacher, the famous Leung Jan.

Master Leung Bik's Wing Chun was much more refined than what Ip Man had learned from Master Chan. While Chan Wah Shun had been a big man, Leung Bik was much smaller. There was also a pretty wide gap in the education level between the two masters. Chan Wah Shun was not very well educated, while Leung Bik was the son of Leung Jan, who was a well educated doctor of Chinese medicine. This education was passed to his son. This meant that Leung Bik was better able to understand the underlying principles of the Wing Chun system. This knowledge was passed to Ip Man.

Upon learning all that Leung Bik had to teach him, Ip Man went on to explore ways to simplify Wing Chun, making it easier to understand. In addition to his education in "Wing Chun", Ip Man received an advanced formal education in his youth. He learned the theories and principles of modern science and could therefore make use of modern technological knowledge such as mechanical and mathematical theories to explain the principles of Wing Chun. Ip Man even changed terminology such as "The Five Elements", and "Eight Diagrams" (Ba Gua) which were commonly used in metaphysics. This helped to demystify Wing Chun, thus making it easier for the common student to understand and apply the system.

After completing his Wing Chun education under Leung Bik, Ip Man returned to China. Back in Foshan, Ip Man began teaching a small group of students, including Kwok Fu and Luen Kai. In 1949 Ip Man returned to live in Hong Kong, where he eventually began his public instruction of Wing Chun.

In July 1950, through Lee Man's introduction, Grandmaster Ip Man started teaching in Dai Lam Street, Kowloon. The first Wing Chun Kung Fu class was for the Restaurant Workers Association. When he opened the class there was only 8 people, including Leung Shang and Lok Yiu. All these were restaurant workers, but later he was joined by Chu Shung Tin, Yip Bo Ching, Chiu Wan, Lee Yan Wing, Law Peng, Man Siu Hung, and others. Grandmaster Ip Man also taught in the Restaurant Workers Shang Wan branch, Union HQ in Hong Kong. Students included Lee Wing, Yue May Keng, Lee Leung Foon, and others.

Ip Man training on the Wooden Dummy. Taken during the filming of the 8MM made for his sons just 10 days prior to his death in 1972.

Over the next 20 years Ip Man would leave his mark on the world of martial arts by teaching those that would spread Wing Chun across the globe. Some of those who became students of the Grandmaster were Wong Shun Leung, Bruce Lee, and of course Ip Man's sons, Ip Chun and Ip Ching.

The Ip Man Wing Chun system has today become one of the most popular martial art systems in the world. Bruce Lee was initially responsible for bringing Wing Chun to the attention of the world, but it has been through the teaching of today's masters, and most notably Ip Man's sons Ip Chun and Ip Ching that we have full knowledge of the heritage of this great Kung Fu system.

Wing Chun History
by Ip Man

The founder of the Ving Tsun (Wing Chun) Kung Fu System, Miss Yim Ving Tsun was a native of Canton China. As a young girl, she was intelligent and athletic, upstanding and manly. She was betrothed to Leung Bok Chau, a salt merchant of Fukien. Soon after that, her mother died. Her father, Yim Yee, was wrongfully accused of a crime, and nearly went to jail. So the family moved far away, and finally settled down at the foot of Tai Leung Mountain at the Yunnan-Szechuan border. There, they earned a living by selling bean curd. All this happened during the reign of Emperor K'anghsi (1662-1722).

At the time, Kung Fu was becoming very strong in Siu Lam Monastery (Shaolin Monastery) of Mt. Sung, Honan. This

Grandmaster Ip Man training with his knives. These knives now belong to Master Samuel Kwok, part of the heritage passed to him by Grandmaster Ip Ching.

aroused the fear of the Manchu government, which sent troops to attack the Monastery. They were unsuccessful. A man called Chan Man Wai was the First Placed Graduate of the Civil Service Examination that year. He was seeking favour with the government, and suggested a plan. He plotted with Siu Lam monk Ma Ning Yee and others. They set fire to the Monastery while soldiers attacked it from the outside. Siu Lam was burnt down, and the monks scattered. Buddhist Abbess Ng Mui, Abbot Chi Shin, Abbot Pak Mei, Master Fung To Tak and Master Miu Hin escaped and fled their separate ways.

Ng Mui took refuge in White Crane Temple on Mt. Tai Leung (also known as Mt. Chai Har). There she came to know Yim Yee and his daughter Yim Ving Tsun. She bought bean curds at their store. They became friends.

Ving Tsun was a young woman then, and her beauty attracted the attention of a local bully. He tried to force Ving Tsun to marry him. She and her father were very worried. Ng Mui learned of this and took pity on Ving Tsun. She agreed to teach Ving Tsun fighting techniques so that she could protect herself. Then she would be able to solve the problem with the bully, and marry Leung Bok Chau, her betrothed husband. So Ving Tsun followed Ng Mui into the mountains, and started to learn Kung Fu. She trained night and day, and mastered the techniques. Then she challenged the local bully to a fight and beat him. Ng Mui set off to travel around the country, but before she left, she told Ving Tsun to strictly honour the Kung Fu traditions, to develop her Kung Fu after her marriage, and to help the people working to overthrow the Manchu government and restore the Ming Dynasty. This is how Ving Tsun Kung Fu was handed down by Abbess Ng Mui. After the marriage, Ving Tsun taught her Kung Fu to her husband Leung Bok Chau, and he passed his Kung Fu techniques on to Leung Lan Kwai. Leung Lan Kwai passed it on to Wong Wah Bo. Wong Wah Bo was a member of an opera troupe on board a junk, known to the Chinese as the Red Junk. Wong worked on the Red Junk with Leung Yee Tei. It so happened that Abbot Chi Shin, who fled from Siu Lam, had disguised himself as a cook and was now working on the Red Junk. Chi Shin taught the Six-and-a-half Point Long Pole Techniques to Leung Yee Tei. Wong Wah Bo was close to Leung Yee Tei, and they shared what they knew about Kung Fu. Together they correlated and improved their techniques, and thus the Six-and-half-point Long Pole Techniques were incorporated into Ving Tsun Kung Fu.

Leung Yee Tei passed the Kung Fu on to Leung Jan, a well known herbal doctor in Fat Shan/Foshan. Leung Jan grasped the innermost secrets of Ving Tsun, and attained the highest level of proficiency. Many Kung Fu masters came to challenge him, but all were defeated. Leung Jan became very famous. Later, he passed his Kung Fu on to Chan Wah Shan, who took me as his student many decades ago. I studied Kung Fu alongside my Kung Fu brothers such as Ng Siu Lo, Ng Chung So, Chan Yu Min and Lui Yu Jai. Ving Tsun was thus passed down to us, and we are eternally grateful to our Kung Fu ancestors and teachers.

We will always remember and appreciate our roots, and this shared feeling will always keep our Kung Fu brothers close together. This is why I am organizing the Ving Tsun Fellowship, and I hope my Kung Fu brothers will support me in this. This will be very important in the promotion of Kung Fu.

CHAPTER 2

Basic Principles

In order to gain the full benefit of training on the Wooden Dummy, the trainee needs to understand the foundation principles of Wing Chun. That is why it is said that the Wooden Dummy training should not be undertaken until the student has developed at least a rather advanced understanding of Siu Lim Tao and Chum Kiu level Wing Chun.

Wing Chun is a very practical system guided by a set of underlying principles which form the theoretical foundation of the system. A basic understanding of the following principles will help the student in their pursuit of mastery of the Wooden Dummy form

Centerline

The centerline principle is at the foundation of most Wing Chun techniques. The protection of your own centerline and the attack of the opponent's centerline are at the very heart of Wing Chun methodology. In training the Wooden Dummy form the trainee will have to remain aware of the centerline throughout the transitions from one movement to another. The trainee will have to understand how the stepping, angling, and shifting changes the centerline position in relation to the Dummy. It is, this training which sharpens the trainee's understanding of the proper application of his structure against an opponent, and how to use position and angle to the greatest advantage in a fight.

Most of the body's vital areas lie directly on or within a few inches to either side of the centerline. This makes the protection of one's own centerline of vital importance, and attack of the opponent's centerline of strategic value. (Graphic Centerline 1)

Proper training of Siu Lim Tao level Wing Chun will build the conditioned reflex of protecting the centerline. The Chum Kiu form will teach how your movement relates to that of an opponent. It is these two keys from the forms that will be perfected in the Wooden Dummy training. The Dummy becomes the opponent. You will, through the Dummy training, develop a mastery of keeping your vital areas guarded in the dynamic environment of stepping, and shifting. It is through the Dummy training that the trainee will learn to keep the line directly between himself and the Dummy covered at all times, thus improving his ability to defend himself in a real fighting situation.

Theory of Facing

In the theory of facing, the Wing Chun fighter can face the opponent squarely. In Western Boxing and several other systems the fighter will have one hand/shoulder as the forward or lead side. In Wing Chun's method, the fighter can react equally with either hand and is not restricted in reach or range of motion by starting with one side forward and the other back. Even if the Wing Chun fighter has one leg as the lead leg, the upper body can still remain square, so, in Wing Chun, a lead leg does not mean a lead side. The square "nature" of Wing Chun's facing posture makes protection of the centerline much easier and natural. In training on the Wooden Dummy, the trainee will feel the posture and structure of his own technique when contact is made. It is the feedback the trainee gets from training with the Wooden Dummy that solidifies the understanding of the importance of proper position and structure of technique. (Graphic Facing 2)

This enables the Wing Chun practitioner to spring into a leading stance on either side of the attack, with proper structure, thus making Wing Chun a flexible and effective fighting system.

Gates, Doors, and Zones

Wing Chun divides the body into a matrix of areas in order to understand effective attacking and protective methods. When you look at the body as it is facing you, the centerline divides the body into two equal halves. The outside shoulder lines form the outer boundary lines. The area inside the outside shoulder lines is considered the "Indoor Area". Outside the shoulder line is considered the "Outdoor Area". (Graphic Centerline 3)

Training on the Wooden Dummy follows the aforementioned principles and helps the trainee develop an understanding of position in relation to these defined

areas. The trainee will be constantly be moving from indoor area, to outdoor area and back, throughout the Dummy training set. This constant changing of position in association to the Dummy will make understanding the relationship of the defensive and offensive tools of Wing Chun more clear to the trainee. Understanding these boundary lines becomes important in applying attacks and in the understanding of proper defensive techniques. For example, if the opponent applies a straight punch, a defensive maneuver which applies a block from the "Outdoor Area" will be much safer than one from the "Indoor Area", as you will not be in immediate reach of the opponents other hand. Also, the "Outdoor Area" block has an excluding or jamming effect on the opponent's non-punching hand. The body is also divided into upper, middle, and lower areas known as "Gates". This helps define the

proper tool to use in protection of the body against attack, as well as helping in the understanding of properly directed attack. For example, Wing Chun generally keeps it's kicking attacks at, or below the waist line, which forms the upper boundary line of the "Lower Gate". It is the belief in Wing Chun that to kick above the "Lower Gate" will leave you off balance and vulnerable to attacks to your own "Lower Gate" during any kick above this target area on the opponent. Although high kicks can be powerful they leave you vulnerable, hence Wing Chun keeps its kicks low. The trainee will find that all of the kicks performed in the Wooden Dummy set are to targets of waist height or lower. The remaining portion of the matrix is that of "Zones". This is the portion of the matrix that teaches about the

reach of our offensive weapons and defensive tools. The area of our reach is divided into three zones. Zone one is the extreme outskirts of our reach. In attack, we can see that in this zone the opponent is outside the reach of all of our upper weapons with the exception of our fingertips. Zone one is primarily one of "Kicking Range". (Graphic Zones 4)

In zone two the opponent will be vulnerable to your knee, punch, palm, and Fak Sao, as well as still being in range of the zone one weapons. Zone three is for close range weapons use. Many of the attacks used in zones one and two will not be very effective at this range as it is too close to use proper structure to generate power. Techniques such as elbow and shoulder strikes will be used in this zone. The Wing Chun practitioner has a wide repertoire of different elbow strikes that can be used. These include Kop Jarn or downwards elbow strike as seen in the image above. This technique makes up a large part of Wing Chun's third form. The Wing Chun practitioner

can also use Pie Jarn, which is a horizontal elbow strike developed in Chum Kiu. The power of Wing Chun elbows can be devastating. Defensively, zones are used to explain the effective tools for blocking. In zone one, the hands and legs are used defensively.

In zone two, the forearm is the primary tool of defense through the use of Biu Sao, Bong Sao, Jaum Sao, Tan Sao, and a number of other defensive techniques. Zone three is primarily one of trapping the opponent's hands for defense. However, techniques such as the strike Kop Jarn can also be used defensively at extremely close range to block an opponents attack. Other techniques such as Kwan Sao or rotating arms, can be use to free ones self from a trap in this zone.

Wing Chun Stances and Stepping

Siu Lim Tao Ma – The Center Balance Stance

This is the basic starting posture of the Dummy form. It is the stance from Wing Chun's first form and has a weight distribution of 50 / 50. This is the center – facing posture and is used as a starting and ending point of the Dummy sections. This is also a transitional posture during some of the movements of the Dummy form.

Chor Ma or Chum Kiu Ma

This is the side weighted stance which is created in shifting the weight to either side out of the Siu Lim Tao Ma. This shifting develops power in the Wing

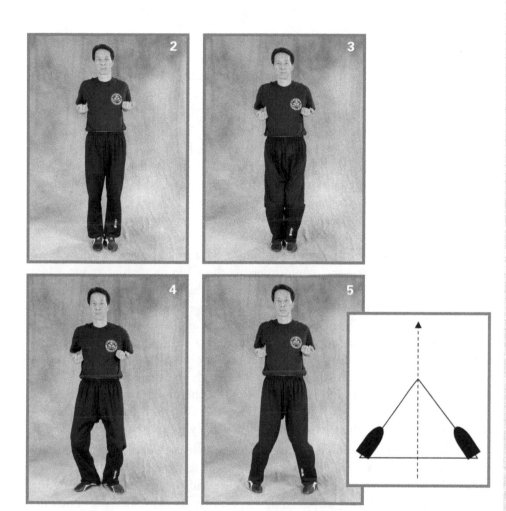

Chun movements and creates a different angle in relation to the Dummy from that of the Siu Lim Tao Ma. The shifting stance can be used from facing one side, back to the center facing position or is sometimes used in transition from one side all the way over to the opposite side.

Biu Ma

Biu Ma or thrusting stance is used to refer to the kind of stance and footwork developed in Chum Kiu. Wing Chun's stepping is designed to give its practitioner maximum stability, whilst maintaining maximum security from attack. The basic position of one's feet when using Biu Ma is as follows: Feet are approximately shoulders width apart or slightly over, and the feet are at 45 degrees. The power for the stepping comes from ankle strength built through the Achilles tendon, as well as leg strength. The power for the step is driven from the back leg. The practitioner should direct power down into the ground with the back leg, and then thrust the power out, remembering to move the front leg first. Always check the

position of the feet when in place. Do not leave the feet too close together or too far apart. A common mistake is to stand on your toes, but this prevents the generation of extra power in the step, and also compromises the structure of the practitioner.

In order to give the practitioner maximum stability, whilst maintaining maximum security from attack the feet should be slightly over shoulders width apart as this gives maximum stability. Further apart and the balance is too spread and the legs become very vulnerable targets. Any closer and the legs have little balance as all your weight is balancing on a small area. Feet should be at approximately 45 degrees and parallel. If they are both square on in a forward direction, they are immobile, and if they are square on at any direction they expose the knee joint and shin area to attack. It will also inhibit the practitioner when changing direction to deal with an attack from the side or behind if the feet are square on. The knees should also be slightly bent, conforming to the Chinese martial saying which warns that "A straight leg is a broken leg." Also when the legs are bent, they are like a coiled spring ready to move. Almost all of the practitioner's weight should be on the back leg, which enables for a fast advance and retreat as one leg is thrusting forward, back or to the side. This also means weight does not have to be shifted to kick with the front leg as it can move without disrupting the balance, or telegraphing the intention to kick. Therefore, with the weight on the back leg, front kicks can be performed easily and swiftly. Furthermore, having weight on the back leg prevents an attack to the front leg being as dangerous to your balance. This is useful because the front leg is the most likely to be attacked.

The feet should be flat on the floor when stationary as opposed to being up on the toes as this gives a more stable surface on which to fight. Standing on your toes is like fighting on stilts. The feet should be flat and only push up onto the toes when pushing off during stepping. Once the step is complete, the foot must always be firmly rooted to the ground.

Seep Ma

Seep Ma is a step that intercepts the fighting line of the opponent. It is used to step around and back in to the opponents center. This is a movement which is used quite often in the Dummy form.

Huen Ma

Huen Ma or "circling stance" is the stance and footwork that is developed in the 3rd form, Biu Gee. Huen Ma is extremely effective when combined with the footwork of Biu Ma. Huen Ma enables the practitioner to shift weight and change position quickly and safely. The Huen Ma is a very flexible movement and can be used and applied in a multitude of different ways. It can be used to aggressively receive attacks or to circle around your opponent to attack them from a different angle. It can also be used to maneuver safely when fighting multiple opponents.

Yiu Ma

Yiu Ma teaches waist energy. This principle should be present in all of Wing Chun's footwork. Yiu Ma is present when the step, the body and the hand technique is coordinated with the idea of creating dynamic power. According to Grandmaster Ip Ching, "Yiu Ma is the real secret to Wing Chun's power".

Two Way Energy and the Lap Sao

Two way energy sounds like a complex term. However it is simply referring to the way a Wing Chun practitioner can use their opponent's force against them. A

prime example of this is when the practitioner combines a Lap Sao with a strike. The Lap Sao can be a continuation of the force of the opponent's punch; when combined with a strike like a Fak Sao the other way, the result is a greater impact. Another way of looking at this is to imagine an object like a car moving at 30 miles an hour. If it hits an object that is standing still it will do a certain amount of damage. However, if it hits another car moving in the opposite direction, the collision and damage will be dramatically increased.

The practitioner uses the stance as a pivot point, so if for example the left side of the body performs a Lap Sao, then the stance turns away from the opponent on the left side. The result of this is that the right side of the body moves forward. This forward motion can be used to add power to the strike. One of the benefits of this kind of two direction energy is that it enables the practitioner to deliver a strike that is much more powerful than would be delivered by just the strike alone. (Graphic Lap 1)

When using two way energy the practitioner must balance the motion so that it is one smooth movement without a stutter or stopping. This ensures that all the power is unified. A common mistake is to pull when performing the Lap Sao. This prevents two way energy as a pull places all the force in one direction. Instead, the Lap Sao should be powered by the turning in the stance. The practitioner should use the Yiu Ma or waist energy. This is difficult to master however, once the practitioner develops the generation of power coming from their stance, they will be able to Lap Sao much bigger and stronger opponents with a coordinated strike which can be devastating.

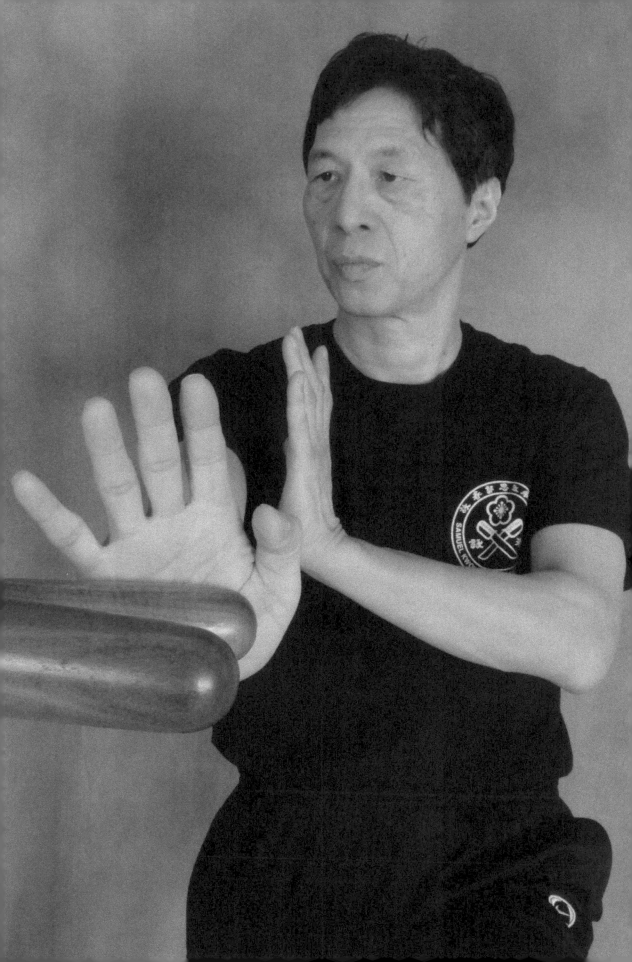

CHAPTER 3

Martial Sayings of Wing Chun

There are many traditions in the Chinese Martial Arts. One such tradition is that the principles are passed in an oral tradition through sayings or proverbs which capture the essence of the system. The following are Wing Chun proverbs which have been passed down to our generation from the warriors of the past. These sayings, sometimes called "Kune Kuit" which in Cantonese means "Martial Sayings" or "Fighting Songs", explain the keys to Wing Chun. There are sayings about moral conduct (Mo Duk), about the system as a whole, and about the individual forms. The list here is not all of the sayings, but some of the more relevant sayings for the Wooden Dummy level of training.

These Wing Chun proverbs are wonderful reminders to the keys to the mastery of this fighting art. The authors do not take credit for this list of sayings. They are oral traditions of Wing Chun. The original author or authors are unknown.

TRADITIONAL WING CHUN RULES OF CONDUCT

Remain disciplined–Conduct yourself ethically as a martial artist.

Practice courtesy and righteousness–Serve the society and respect your elders.

Love your fellow students–Be united and avoid conflicts.

Limit your desires and pursuit of bodily pleasures–Preserve the proper spirit.

Train diligently–Maintain your skills.

Learn to develop spiritual tranquility–Abstain from arguments and fights.

Participate in society–Be moderate and gentle in you manners.

Help the weak and the very young–Use martial skills for the good of humanity.

Pass on the tradition–Preserve this Chinese art and rules of conduct.

MAXIMS OF WING CHUN

The novice fights across the stream, the master fights from the bridge.

If there is no bridge, build one.

Retain what's coming in, follow what is retreating. Thrust in upon loss of hand contact.

Do not chase the hands past the release.

Do not be lax when your opponent is not advancing.

Once your opponent moves,, his center changes.

Others walk the bow, we walk the string.

Make the first move to have control. Attack according to timing.

Timing is achieved through practice.

A strong attitude and posture gives an advantage over your opponent.

Being alert and adapting to the situation allows maximum results for minimum effort.

The body follows the movement of the hands. The waist and the stance move together.

Complement the hands with posture to make good use of the centerline.

The eyes and the mind travel together, paying attention to leading edge of attack.

Charge into the opponent. Execute three moves together.

Strike any presented posture if it is there. Otherwise strike where you see motion. Beware of sneak attacks, leakage attacks and invisible centerline attacks.

Soft and relaxed strength will put your opponent in jeopardy.

Coordinate the hands and feet. Movement is together.

Do not take risks and you will always connect to the target.

Have confidence and your calmness will dominate the situation.

Occupy the inner gate to strike deep into the defense.

To win in an instant is a superior achievement.

The Yin Yang principle should be thoroughly understood.

The theory of Wing Chun has no limit in it applications.

Be humble to request your teacher for guidance.

Understand the principles for your training.

Upon achieving the highest level of proficiency,

The application of techniques will vary according to the opponent.

WING CHUN TRAINING PROVERBS

There are not many sets of training exercises in Wing Chun.

They are easy to learn but to master them requires determination.

Learning the usual ways will allow later variations.

Short arm bridges and fast steps requires practicing the stance first.

Siu Lim Tau mainly trains internal power.

Lon Sau in Chum Kiu is a forceful technique.

Bui Jee contains life saving emergency techniques.

The Wooden Man develops use of power and structure.

Fancy techniques should not be used in sticky hand practice.

The steps follow turning of the body like a cat.

The posture complements the hands to eject the opponent.

The Six and a Half Point Staff does not make more than one sound.

The Eight Cut Sword techniques have no match.

The thrusting and fast attacks are well suited for closing in.

Eyes beaming with courage can neutralize the situation.

Those who completely master the system are among the very few.

SEVENTEEN KEYS TO WING CHUN

Fight from the bridge

Be ferocious when clashing.

Be fast with your fist.

Be relaxed when applying power.

Be accurate with timing.

Be continuous when applying Fak Sau.

Do not use all your strength.

Protect your own posture.

Be alert with your eyes.

Unite you waist and stance.

Coordinate your hands and feet.

Movements must be agile.

Comprehend the principles of Yin and Yang.

Remain calm.

Be steady with your breathing and strength.

Be commanding with your fighting demeanor.

Be quick to end the fight.

YEE JEE KIM YEUNG MA (Siu Lim Tao Ma)

Pull in the chest, push out the upper back, and bring in the tail bone.

Fill the Tan Tien with Ch'i and distribute the strength to all parts of the body.

Point the knees and toes inward.

Form a pyramid with the center of gravity in the center.

Fists are placed by the side of the ribs but not touching the body.

Sink the elbows, the shoulders, and the waist.

Hold the head and neck straight and keep the spirit alert.

Eyes are level, looking straight ahead, and watching all directions.

The mind is free of distractions and the mood is bright.

There is no fear when facing the opponent.

Yee Jee Kim Yeung Ma is the main stance.

Develop a good foundation for advanced techniques.

SIU LIM TAU

Siu Lim Tau comes first.

Do not force progress in training.

A weak body must start with strength improvement.

Do not keep any bad habit.

Train the Ch'i by controlling the Tan Tien.

To maintain good balance of strength, grip the ground with the toes.

To release Ch'i from the Tan Tien, will enable proper release of power.

Sink the elbow and drop the shoulders, guarding the centerline to protect both flanks.

There are one hundred and eight moves, all practical and real.

Thousands of variations can be used.

Aiming for practical use and not beauty.

Internally develop the Ch'i, externally train the tendons, bones and muscles.

Taun Sau, Bong Sau, Fok Sau, Wu Sau, and Huen Sau, their wonder grows with practice.

Each movement must be clear and crisp.

Timing must be observed.

Practice once a day, more will cause no harm.

CHUM KIU

Chum Kiu trains the stance and the waist.

The arm bridge is short and the step is narrow.

Eyes are trained to be alert.

The Ch'i flows in a perpetual motion.

Strive to remain calm in the midst of motion.

Loosen up the muscles and relax the mind.

Turning the stance with a circular movement, will allow superior generation of power.

When the opponent's arm bridge enters my arm bridge, use the escaping hand to turn around the situation.

Pass by the opponent's incoming arm bridge from above, without stopping when the countering move has started.

Lon Sau and Jip Sau, put an opponent in danger.

Do not collide with a strong opponent, with a weak opponent use a direct frontal assault.

A quick fight should be ended quickly, no delay can be allowed.

Use the three joints of the arm to prevent entry by the opponent's bridge.

Jam the opponent's bridge to restrict his movement.

Create a bridge if the opponent's bridge is not present.

Nullify the bridge according to how it is presented.

The arm bridge tracks the movement of the opponent's body.

When the hands cannot prevail, use body position to save the situation.

Using short range power to jam the opponent's bridge.

The three joints are nicely controlled.

Where is the opponent's bridge to be found?

Chum Kiu guides the way.

BIU JEE

The Biu Jee hand contains emergency techniques.

Iron fingers can strike a vital point at once.

The stepping in elbow strike has sufficient threatening power.

Fak Sau, and Guide Bridge, their movements are closely coordinated and hard to defend and nullify.

Springy power and the extended arm are applied to close range.

The situation is different when preventing from defeat in an emergency.

The Biu Jee is not taught to outsiders.

How many Sifu pass on the proper heritage?

THE WOODEN MAN (Mook Jong)

There are 108 movements for the Wooden Man.

Repeated practice brings proper use of power.

Steps vary and always maintain close contact with the Wooden Man.

Power starts from the heart and shoots towards the centerline of Mok Yan Jong.

Up, down, back and forth, the movements are continuous.

Power improvement cannot be predicted.

The arm bridge sticks to the hands of the Wooden Man while moving.

Adhesion power when achieved will be a threatening force.

Power can be released in the intended manner.

Use of the line and position will be proper and hard to defeat.

Wing Chun Code of Conduct

The Wing Chun Code of Conduct said to have originated with Leung Jan and passed to the current generation by Ip Man, serves as a reminder to all practitioners that their martial art represents more than just fighting. It requires the acceptance of a strong moral philosophy framed in courage, honor, ethics and humble etiquette. Wing Chun must be preserved for warriors, not bullies and braggarts. Living this "Code of Honor" is the way of the warrior.

This is the marble display of the Code of Conduct that hangs at the Hong Kong Athletic Association.

守 紀 律 崇 尚 武 德
sáu géi leuht súhng seuhng móuh dāk
Remain disciplined – uphold yourself ethically as a martial artist

明 禮 義 愛 國 尊 親
mìhng láih yih ngoi gwok jyūn chān
Practice courtesy and righteousness – serve the community and honor your family

愛 同 學 團 結 樂 群
ngoi tùhng hohk tyùhn git lohk kwahn
Love your fellow students or classmates – be united and avoid conflicts

節 色 慾 保 守 精 神
jit sīk yuhk bóu sáu jīng sàhn
Limit your desires and pursuit of bodily pleasures – preserve the proper spirit

勤 練 習 技 不 離 身
kàhn lihn jaahp geih bāt lèih sān
Train diligently and make it a habit – maintain your skills

學 養 氣 救 濫 鬥 民
hohk yéuhng hei gau laahm dau màhn
Learn to develop spiritual tranquility – abstain from arguments and fights

常 處 世 態 度 溫 民
sèyhng chyu sai taai douh wān màhn
Participate in society – be conservative, cultured and gentle in your manners

扶 弱 小 以 武 輔 仁
fùh yeuhk siu yih móuh fuh yàhn
Help the weak and the very young – use your martial skill for the good of humanity

繼 光 緒 漢 持 祖 訓
gai gwōng séuih hon chìh jóu fan
Pass on the tradition – preserve this Chinese art and its Rules of Conduct

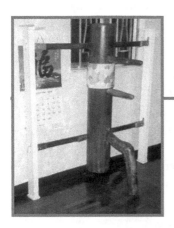

CHAPTER 4

Mok Yan Jong
The Perfect
Training Partner

Wing Chun is well known for several unique training methods and applications. Principles such as the center line, simultaneous defense and attack, Chi Sao or "sticking hands" and the famous Wooden Dummy or Mook Yan Jong. The Wooden Man Dummy as it is commonly known is a very unique training device. It is comprised of a body, three arms and a leg. Unlike other training devices such as the boxing heavy bag, the Dummy can be utilized to train both defensive and offensive movements. The 116 techniques that comprise the Dummy form, as taught by the late Grandmaster Ip Man, make up an important part of the Wing Chun system. The "Dummy Form" is often said to contain the fighting techniques of the Wing Chun system. This means that the techniques learned in the three empty hand forms are performed against the "Jong" or Dummy, and are therefore being practiced in a way that applies them directly. This is a way of testing the

skills learned in the empty hand forms. The Dummy form is a way of giving impact or collision training to what is learned in the forms. This is because the techniques are performed against the physical arms, legs, and body of the Wooden Dummy. Therefore, the practitioner learns how to deal with impact and collision against a solid object such as an opponent. While this is not the primary reason for training on the Wooden Dummy, it is a added benefit.

The Wooden Dummy itself represents a physical opponent; its arms can represent attacks that have to be blocked, or obstacles for the practitioner to overcome in order to attack the trunk of the Dummy. The leg of the Dummy has to be maneuvered around and attacked by the practitioner during the form. This is where the Wing Chun practitioner gets the opportunity to train fighting footwork.

The advantages of training on a Wooden Dummy are:

- Unlike a live partner, It can be hit as hard as the practitioner wishes.

- It can be trained on for long hours, whereas a live partner might get bored.

- Because the Dummy does not move much, the practitioner learns mobility while circling around the Dummy in conjunction with blocking and striking hand techniques.

The Dummy form contains applications from the three hand forms, along with some additional techniques like the neck pull and some additional kicks. Because of the angle and structure of the Dummy, the techniques of the trainee are refined and angles corrected by the feedback one gets from contact and "fitting in" with the

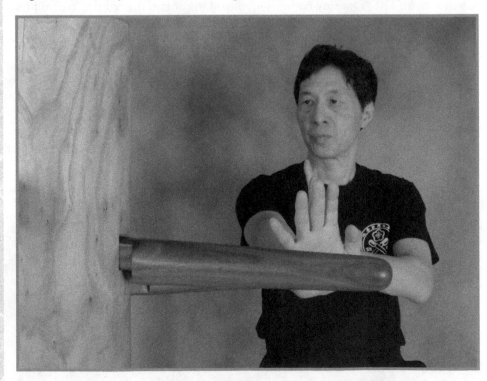

Dummy, any mistakes in the practitioner's technique like incorrect angle, position of a block, or the wrong use of energy, are easily identifiable as it will result in a loss of balance or a clash of force causing pain. One mistake in the positioning of a block in the Dummy form will often lead to the next move being harder to perform. Eventually, positioning and use of energy becomes perfect from training on the Dummy. In working with a live partner there is more than one person moving, so if a mistake is made, and you wish to perform the technique again, it is hard to determine where the mistake occurred. With the Dummy, you are the only one moving, so it is easy to change your angle and know exactly how your structure reacts. It is like sighting in a rifle. You have a gun rest, a gun and a target.

If you sight your scope, take the shot and find it hit high and to the right, you adjust the scope and take your next shot to see if your adjustment was correct. If on the other hand you adjusted your scope and the target was moved, you could not know if your adjustment worked because more than one adjustment was made, your scope and the target. It is much the same in working with a live partner and the Wooden Dummy. It is this ability to judge yourself in relation to the Wooden Dummy that makes it the perfect training partner.

Introduction to Section One

Section one of the Wooden Dummy introduces several "Keys" to the application of Wing Chun against an opponent. In section one, the student is introduced to the concept of body generation of power through the bending of the knees and the explosive raising movement of the body in coordination with the application of a hand technique.

Generally, there are several ways to generate power in application of a technique. You can shift, turn, step, sink or raise the body in coordination with a technique to multiply the power that the limb alone could generate.

In Wing Chun, there is a power generated by the waist energy called Yiu Ma. Yiu Ma can be done with a dynamic shift without stepping or from a coordination of stepping with a dynamic shift during the application of technique. The trainee is introduced to this "Key" concept in the first section of the Dummy.

There are many steps and transitions in the performance of this section. Care should be taken to minimize unnecessary movement, such as, uneconomical movements of the limbs between movements. One of the "Key" elements to learn from this section is that of sticking close to the Dummy's arms, and moving economically in transition between one movement and the next.

The trainee must be careful to coordinate the step with the application of technique and contact with the Dummy. Proper angle will confirm your good structure. Improper angle will make you acutely aware of bad structure.

Section one is divided into two parts called Section 1-A and Section 1-B in this book. There are some instructors who call these two separate sections, however, as they are basically mirror images of each other, we consider them one section, in two parts. This may seem trivial, but there are those out there in the Wing Chun world who would argue over such things, so we felt the need to clarify. In truth, it does not matter if you call them Section 1-A and 1-B, or call them two separate sections. When all is said and done, you will have learned the entire Wooden Dummy as taught by Ip Man. That is our only goal, and we do not wish to get into trivial argument, which distract from the training of this great system.

Section 1

1. Stand in front of the dummy, assume the Siu Lim Tao Ma (balance stance), extend left hand in Tan Sao to check distance from dummy, then Jong Sao (guard hand), left hand forward and right hand in Wu Sao. Sink the stance and drop the left hand slightly and extend left hand to contact with the right arm of the dummy (inside line). (Have the elbow slightly out to form a greater contact area for the block as if deflecting a punch)

2. Turn with Chum Kiu Ma, sinking the weight on right leg, extend the right hand past the Wooden Dummy face through centerline (potentially palm strike to dummy face on way through) and lap sao the right arm of the dummy with the left hand. Sink further into the stance, pulling the neck and right arm of the dummy forward and downward, (ensuring you sink your elbow into the dummy's center when doing the neck pull).

3. Apply the right arm from your elbow into right Bong Sao on the right arm (inside line) of the dummy (contact area for the block is just above the wrist) and left hand Wu Sao

4. Slide the left foot to the left and, utilizing the Sip Ma movement, slide the right foot round the leg of the dummy and move it into contact with the leg of the dummy. Note the left foot pivots to face the dummy and the right foot is parallel to the left. Simultaneously, keeping the right arm in contact with the right arm of the dummy, roll the right arm under the right arm of the dummy and extend it into Tan Sao on the outside line. Again simultaneously, horizontal palm strike with the left hand to the ribs of the dummy.

5. Applying the Sip Ma, slide the right foot round the leg of the dummy and move it back to the center line of the dummy. Simultaneously, drop the right hand into Gaun Sao on the lower arm of the dummy and bring the left hand up into a high Gaun Sao on the outside line of the right arm of the dummy.

6. Utilizing the Biu Ma, slide the right foot to the right and collapse the left arm (bending at the elbow) and extend into a low Bong Sao on the lower arm of the dummy. Simultaneously extend the right arm into Tan Sao on the inside line of the left arm of the dummy (Kwan Sao)

7. Slide the right foot to the right and utilizing the Sip Ma, slide the left foot round the leg of the dummy and move it into contact with the leg of the dummy. Note the right foot pivots to face the dummy and the left foot is parallel to the right. Simultaneously, bring the left arm up to Tan Sao on the outside line of the left arm of the dummy and horizontal palm strike to the ribs of the dummy.

8. Utilizing the Sip Ma, slide the left foot round the leg of the dummy and move it back to the center line of the dummy. Simultaneously, drop the left hand into Gaun Sao on the lower arm of the dummy and bring the right hand up into a high Gaun Sao on the outside line of the left arm of the dummy.

9. Utilizing Chum Kiu Ma transfer the weight to the left leg and slide left leg in line with the right arm of the dummy, simultaneously performing a Huen Sao with the right hand on the left arm of the dummy and bringing the left hand up to Tan Sao on the outside line of the right arm of the dummy.

10. Transferring the weight back to the center in Siu Lim Tao Ma, simultaneously Jut Sao with the left hand on the right hand of the dummy and vertical palm strike the face of the dummy with the right hand.

11. Drop the right hand back to perform a double Jut Sao on the upper arms of the dummy.

12. The hands slide under the upper arms and perform a double Tok Sao.

13. Drop back to Jong Sao, right hand forward.

Top View

1. Jong Sao
2. Mon Sao
3 & 4 . Deflecting Hand and Palm Strike & Neck Sinking hand.
5. Bong/Wu Sao
6 – 8. Step to outside gate, Taun Sao / Low-Side Palm.
9. Step to Gaun Sao.
10. Step to Kwan Sao

Top View

Top View

11. Step to Outside Taun Sao / Low Side Palm.

12. Step to Gaun Sao

13. Shift to a Huen Sao / Taun Sao

14. Jut Sao / Straight Palm

15. Double Jut Sao

Top View

Top View

Top View

Top View

Top View

木人椿

47

13

14

15

Top View

Top View

Top View

16

17

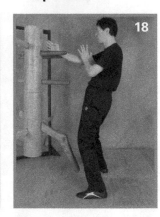

18

Top View

16 . Double Tok Sao

17 – 18. Back to Jong Sao

Section One is completed by performing the same set of movements on the opposite side, with the only change being the straight palm strike in movement 14 is replaced by a low side palm to the dummy's body.

19. Jong Sao

20. Deflecting Hand and Palm Strike & Neck Sinking hand.

21. Bong/Wu Sao

22. Step to outside gate, Taun Sao / Low-Side Palm.

23. Step to Gaun Sao.

24. Step to Kwan Sao

25. Step to Outside Taun Sao / Low Side Palm.

26. Step to Gaun Sao

27. Shift to a Huen Sao / Taun Sao

28. Jut Sao / Low Side Palm

29. Double Jut Sao

30 . Double Tok Sao

48

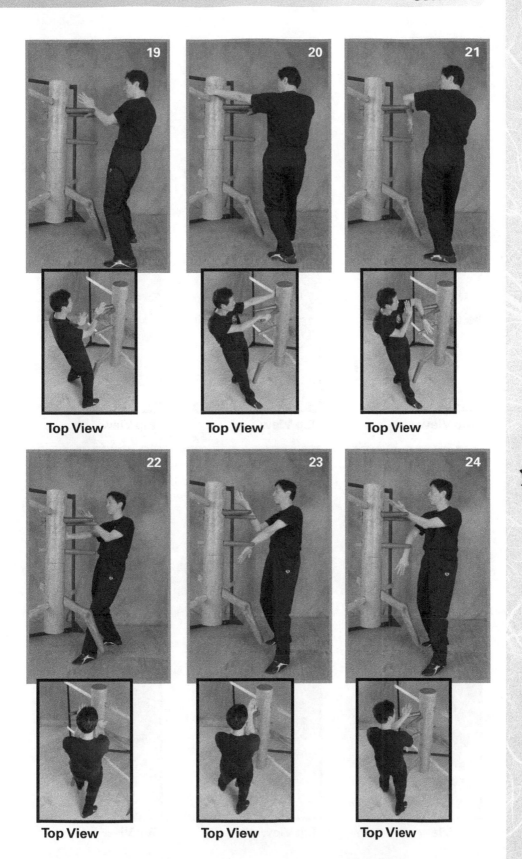

Top View

Top View

Top View

Top View

Top View

Top View

木人椿

49

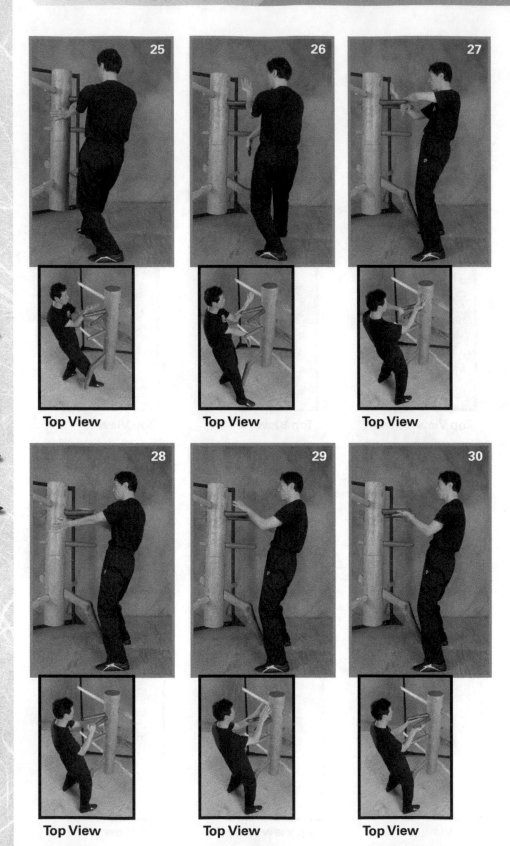

Top View

Top View

Top View

Top View

Top View

Top View

Section 1 NOTES _____

Introduction to Section Two

Section Two of the Wooden Dummy introduces several important elements. In this section, the techniques of Pak Sao, Fak Sao, Dai Bong Sao, and the first dummy kick, Wang Girk are introduced. This section also introduces one of the principles of distance or zone training. The side kick is a kick which is delivered from a greater distance than that of other Wing Chun kicks. So, during the application of the side kick the student must judge the proper distance.

This section of the form also presents the challenge of regaining posture and position when recovering from delivering the kick. This can be difficult, but with training, it can be mastered. In delivering the kick, the Dummy will let you know if you have a good root in your footwork. If you are off balance the Dummy will rebound your energy back to you and cause you to lose your balance.

Section 2

1. Shift to right Chum Kiu Ma, transferring the weight to the right leg and Pak Sao the inside right arm of the dummy with the right hand, left hand Wu Sao.

2. Shift to left Chum Kiu Ma, transferring the weight to the left leg and Pak Sao the inside left arm of the dummy with the left hand, right hand Wu Sao.

3. Shift to right Chum Kiu Ma, transferring the weight to the right leg and Pak Sao the inside right arm of the dummy with the right hand, left hand Wu Sao.

4. Shift to left Chum Kiu Ma, transferring the weight to the left leg and Jut Sao with the left hand on top of the right arm of the dummy from the outside line, right hand Wu Sao.

5. Staying in left stance, strike with Fak Sao to the throat of the dummy with the left hand, right hand Wu Sao.

6. Moving back to Siu Lim Tao Ma, drop the left arm to Pak Sau the top of the left arm of the dummy, simultaneously vertical punch to the body of the dummy with the right hand.

7. Shift to right Chum Kiu Ma, transferring the weight to the right leg and Jut Sao with the right hand on top of the left arm of the dummy from the outside line, left hand Wu Sao.

8. Staying in right stance, strike with Fak Sao to the throat of the dummy with the right hand, left hand Wu Sao.

9. Moving back to Siu Lim Tao Ma, drop the right arm to Pak Sau the top of the right arm of the dummy, simultaneously vertical punch to the body of the dummy with the left hand.

10. Shift to right Chum Kiu Ma, transferring the weight to the right leg and right Bong Sau the lower arm of the dummy (left hand Wu Sao)

11. Step to the left with Biu Ma, while simultaneously performing a left Pak Sau to the outside of the dummy arm and fak sau to the dummy body with the right arm.

12. Cover with Kwan Sau and right leg sideward thrust kick to outside of the right trunk of the dummy (as if kicking a person's ribcage or upper thigh muscle of the leg), In Kwan Sau the right hand is in Bong Sau position and left hand in Wu Sao.

13. Step down from the side kick into Chum Kiu Ma, place the right foot on the floor and maintain the weight on the left leg, simultaneously, with the left hand use the Bong Sau movement on the lower arm (outside line) of the dummy, right hand Wu Sao.

14. Step to the right with Biu Ma, while simultaneously performing a right Pak Sau to the outside of the dummy arm and Fak Sau to the dummy body with the left arm.

15. Cover with Kwan Sau and left leg sideward thrust kick to outside of the left trunk of the dummy (as if kicking a person's ribcage or upper thigh muscle of the leg), In Kwan Sau the left hand is in Bong Sau position and right hand in Wu Sao.

16. Step down from the side kick into Chum Kiu Ma to center line of the dummy. Simultaneously, drop the left hand into low Gaun Sao on the lower arm of the dummy and bring the right hand up into a high Gaun Sao on the outside line of the left arm of the dummy.

17. Utilizing the Chum Kiu Ma shift, transfer the weight to the left leg and slide left leg in line with the right arm of the dummy, simultaneously performing a Huen Sao with the right hand on the left arm of the dummy and bringing the left hand up to Tok Sao under the right arm of the dummy.

18. Transferring the weight back to the center in Siu Lim Tao Ma, simultaneously Jut Sao with the left hand on the right hand of the dummy and vertical palm strike the face of the dummy with the right hand.

19. Staying in Siu Lim Tao Ma, pull downward in a double Jut Sao position

20. Staying in Siu Lim Tao Ma, double Tok Sao under both of the Dummy's arms

1. Jong Sao Guard
2. Right Pak Sao
3. Left Pak Sao
4. Right Pak Sao
5. Left Jut Sao
6. Left Fak Sao

Top View

Top View

Top View

Top View

Top View

7. Left Pak Sao / Right Vertical Punch to body

8. Right Jut Sao

9. Right Fak Sao

10. Right Pak Sao / Left Vertical Punch to body

11. Double Tok Sao

12. Right Low Bong Sao

Top View

Top View

Top View

葉問詠春

56

Top View

Top View

Top View

Top View

Top View

13. Stepping – Left Pak Sao / Right Fak Sao

14. Right Side Kick with Kwan Sao (Bong Sao / Wu Sao) guard

15. Left Low Bong Sao

16. Stepping – Right Pak Sao / Left Fak Sao

17. Left Side Kick with Kwan Sao guard

木人椿

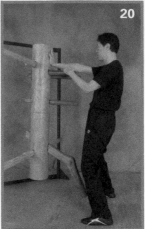

18 **19** **20**

Top View   **Top View**   **Top View**

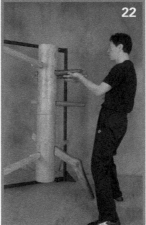

21 **22**

18. High / Low Gaun Sao

19. Right Huen Sao / Left Tok Sao

20. Left Jut Sao / Right Palm Strike

21. Double Jut Sao

22. Double Tok Sao

Top View   **Top View**

Ip Ching Variation

In Ip Ching's method of this section the Pak and Fak Sao application is done with a Biu Ma jamming footwork, and then a backward step for the side kick.

Introduction to Section Three

Section Three of the Wooden Dummy introduces the use of the body raising and sinking to develop power in the strike from a stationary position. This training is very important and must not be neglected if your Kung Fu is to be powerful.

The trainee will encounter the Gaun Sao / Huen Sao combination, coordinated with stance shifting in this section. These movements must be done with dynamic energy, generated by the Yiu Ma (Waist Energy).

Also in this section, the trainee will train the first close range kick of the Dummy set. This is a stomping kick to the Dummy's knee from very close quarters contact. It is important to root your balance on the supporting leg prior to throwing the kick. This will allow the kick to be applied with minimal upper body movement. This develops the Wing Chun principle called "Mo Ying Girk" (No Shadow Kick), sometimes called the invisible kick. The idea here is that in bridge contact with the opponent, the kick can be thrown to a low target area without telegraphing the intent or delivery of the kick to the opponent. When mastered, this is a very devastating skill.

Section 3

1. Staying in Siu Lim Tao stance, double Tan Sau on the outside of the upper arms of the dummy (bend knees and drive upwards with knees at the same time as delivering the double Tan Sau).

2. Staying in Siu Lim Tao stance, double huen sau on the upper arms of the dummy, so that both your arms are inside the upper arms (indoor area), ensure that you keep the elbows in a fixed position (i.e. avoid moving the elbows outwards).

3. Staying in Siu Lim Tao stance, double lower lying palm strikes to the indoor area of the dummy at mid-lower-level (between the upper and lower arm), ensure that you utilize power (by rooting or sinking with the knees) when driving the palm strikes towards the dummy.

4. Staying in Siu Lim Tao stance, double Tan Sau to the upper arms (striking the inside of the arms, i.e. you are the inside line), ensure that you utilize power (by slight upward movement with the knees) when driving the Tan Sau movements towards the dummy.

5. Staying in Siu Lim Tao stance, double upper lying palm strikes to the indoor area of the dummy at upper-level (above the upper arms), ensure that you utilize power (by slight upward movement with the knees) when driving the palm strikes towards the dummy.

6. Staying in Siu Lim Tao stance, double jut sau downwards to the upper arms (striking the outside of the arms, i.e. you are one the outside line), ensure that you utilize power (by slight downward rooting movement with the knees) when driving the jut sau movements towards the arms.

7. Turn to Chum Kiu Ma, weight on left leg, Drop and strike the left hand into Gaun Sao (on the right arm of the dummy) and with the right hand movement is Huen Sao on the inside line of the left arm of the dummy.

8. Turn to Chum Kiu Ma, weight on right leg, raise and strike the right hand into Gaun Sao (on the left arm of the dummy) and with the left hand movement is Huen Sao on the inside line of the right arm of the dummy.

9. Turn to Chum Kiu Ma, weight on left leg, Drop and strike the left hand into Gaun Sao (on the right arm of the dummy) and with the right hand movement is Huen Sao on the inside line of the left arm of the dummy.

10. Transferring the weight back to the center in Siu Lim Tao Ma, simultaneously jut sao with the left hand on the right hand of the dummy and vertical palm strike the face of the dummy with the right hand.

11. Turn to Chum Kiu Ma, weight on right leg, Collapse the right arm from your elbow into right Bong Sao on the right arm (inside line) of the dummy (contact area for the block is just above the wrist).

12. Slide the left foot to the left and, utilizing the circular foot movement (Huen Ma) from Biu Gee, slide the right foot round the leg of the dummy and right knee-stamping kick to the right leg of the dummy. Note the left foot pivots to face the dummy and the right foot is parallel to the left. Simultaneously, keeping the right arm in contact with the right arm of the dummy, roll the right arm under the right arm of the dummy and extend it into Tan Sao on the outside line. Again simultaneously, horizontal palm strike with the left hand to the ribs of the dummy.

13. Utilizing the Huen Ma from Biu Gee, slide the right foot round the leg of the dummy and move it back to the center line of the dummy. Simultaneously, drop the right hand into Gaun Sao on the lower arm of the dummy and bring the left hand up into a high Gaun Sao on the outside line of the right arm of the dummy.

14. Turn to Chum Kiu Ma, weight on right leg, raise and strike the right hand into Gaun Sao (on the left arm of the dummy) and with the left hand movement is Huen Sao on the inside line of the right arm of the dummy.

15. Turn to Chum Kiu Ma, weight on left leg, Drop and strike the left hand into Gaun Sao (on the right arm of the dummy) and the right hand movement is Huen Sao on the inside line of the left arm of the dummy.

16. Turn to Chum Kiu Ma, weight on right leg, raise and strike the right hand into Gaun Sao (on the left arm of the dummy) and with the left hand movement is Huen Sao on the inside line of the right arm of the dummy.

17. Transferring the weight back to the center in Siu Lim Tao Ma, simultaneously jut sao with the right hand on the left hand of the dummy and lower lying palm (spade) strike the mid-level of the dummy with the left hand.

18. Turn to Chum Kiu Ma, transfer the weight to the left leg and left Bong Sau the inside line of the upper left arm of the dummy (right hand Wu Sao)

19. Slide the right foot to the right and, utilizing the Huen Ma movement from Biu Gee, slide the left foot round the leg of the dummy and left knee stamping kick to the leg of the dummy. Note the right foot pivots to face the dummy and the left foot is parallel to the right. Simultaneously, keeping the left arm in contact with the left arm of the dummy, roll the left arm under the left arm of the dummy and extend it into Tan Sao on the outside line. Again simultaneously, horizontal palm strike with the right hand to the ribs of the dummy.

20. Place the left foot down after completing the kick and then slide the left foot to the left with weight on right leg, raise and strike the right hand into Gaun Sao (on the left arm of the dummy) and with the left hand Gaun Sao on the lower arm of the dummy.

21. Turn to Chum Kiu Ma, transfer the weight to the other leg, left hand tok sau on right arm of the dummy and right huen sau on the left arm of the dummy

22. Transferring the weight back to the center in Siu Lim Tao Ma, simultaneously jut sao with the left hand on the right hand of the dummy and vertical palm strike the face of the dummy with the right hand.

23. Pull both hands downward in a double Jut Sao position.

24. Finish this section with double Tok Sao movement underneath the arms.

1. Jong Sao
2.& 3. Transition to double outside Taun Sao
4 & 5. double Huen Sao
6. Double Palm Strike

Top View

Top View

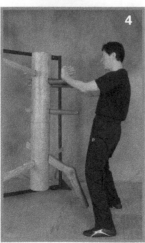

Top View

Top View

Top View

Top View

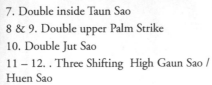

7. Double inside Taun Sao
8 & 9. Double upper Palm Strike
10. Double Jut Sao
11 – 12. . Three Shifting High Gaun Sao /
Huen Sao

Top View

Top View

木人椿

13 – 16. . Three Shifting High Gaun Sao / Huen Sao
17 & 18. Jut Sao / Palm Strike

Top View

Top View

Top View

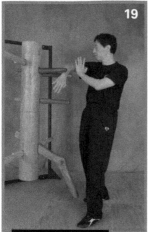

19. Bong / Wu Sao

20 & 21. Transition to Knee Stamping Kick with Taun Sao / Palm Strike

22. High / Low Gaun Sao

23 – 24. Three Shifting High Gaun Sao / Huen Sao

Top View

Top View

Top View

Top View

Top View

25

26

27

Top View

Top View

Top View

28

29

30

24. Three Shifting High Gaun Sao / Huen Sao

26. Right Jut Sao / Left Low Side Palm

27. Bong / Wu Sao

28 & 29. Transition to Knee Stamping Kick with Taun Sao / Palm Strike

30. High / Low Gaun Sao

Top View

Top View

Top View

Top View

Top View

Top View

31 . High Gaun Sao / Huen Sao

32. Left Jut Sao / Right Palm Strike

33. Double Jut Sao

34. Double Tok Sao

木人椿

Introduction to Section Four

Section Four of the Wooden Dummy introduces the concept of "control of the centerline with a single hand". The opening movement utilizes the left and right controlling hand from the Biu Gee form. This principle teaches the method of occupying the centerline and the use of a subtle shifting of the hand to protect against a straight line attack from the opponent.

Also in this section is the Po Pai Jeung. Sometimes called the "Butterfly Palms" because of their shape, these palms are great tools for trapping, and taking the balance of the opponent. You will find the Po Pai Jeung a very useful technique which can be launched from several positions.

The Po Pai can be applied following:

1. Kwan Sao
2. Gaun Sao
3. Bong Sao

In these situations, the transition is minimal making the technique very fast and economical. In application, Po Pai should have a slight upward angle, used to uproot the opponent and steal his balance and stability.

Section 4

1. Remaining in Siu Lim Tao stance, place right hand forward in Jong Sao position and left hand Wu Sao, then flip your right hand to the right arm of dummy (inside line). Ensure you utilize the wrist movement from the opening of the Biu Gee form.

2. Remaining in Siu Lim Tao stance, flip your right hand to the left arm of dummy (inside line) and left hand Wu Sao. Ensure you utilize the wrist movement from the opening of the Biu Gee form.

3. Remaining in Siu Lim Tao stance, flip your right hand back to the right arm of dummy (inside line) and left hand Wu Sao. Ensure you utilize the wrist movement from the opening of the Biu Gee form.

4. Utilizing the shift to Chum Kiu Ma, transfer the weight to the left leg and left hand lower lying palm strike to lower middle part of the dummy and right huen sau on the left arm of the dummy.

5. Collapse the left arm (bending at the elbow) and extend into a low Bong Sao on the lower arm of the dummy. Simultaneously extend the right arm into Tan Sao on the inside line of the left arm of the dummy (Kwan Sao).

6. Returning to Siu Lim Tao Ma, the right hand poses as an erect palm and the left hand poses as a reverse palm, simultaneously strike both palms at the lower middle level of the dummy (Po Pai double palm movement). Remember to extend the knees upwards as driving the palms to the dummy, in order to create more power.

7. Utilizing the shift to Chum Kiu Ma, transfer the weight to the left leg, move the left arm from your elbow into left Bong Sao on the left arm (inside line) of the dummy (contact area for the block is just above the wrist). Right hand is in Wu Sao.

8. Slide the right foot to the right and, utilizing the Sip Ma, slide the left foot round the leg of the dummy and move it into contact with the leg of the dummy. Note the right foot pivots to face the dummy and the left foot is parallel to the right. Simultaneously, the left hand poses as a reverse palm and the right hand poses as an erect palm, strike both palms at the lower middle level of the dummy (Po Pai double palm movement) on the outside line of the dummy. Remember to extend the knees upwards as driving the palms to the dummy, in order to create more power.

9. Utilizing the Biu Ma, slide the left foot round the leg of the dummy and move it back to the center line of the dummy. Simultaneously, raise the right hand into a high Gaun Sao on the upper left arm of the dummy and drop the left hand up into a low Gaun Sao on the outside line of the left lower arm of the dummy.

10. Shifting to Siu Lim Tao Ma, the right hand poses as an erect palm and the left hand poses as a reverse palm, simultaneously strike both palms at the lower middle level of the dummy (Po Pai double palm movement). Remember to extend the knees upwards as driving the palms to the dummy, in order to create more power.

11. Shifting to Chum Kiu Ma, transfer the weight to the right leg, collapse the right arm from your elbow into right Bong Sao on the right arm (inside line) of the dummy (contact area for the block is just above the wrist), left hand in Wu Sao.

12. Slide the left foot to the left and, utilizing the Sip Ma, slide the right foot round the leg of the dummy and move it into contact with the leg of the dummy. Note the left foot pivots to face the dummy and the right foot is parallel to the left. Simultaneously, the left hand poses as an erect palm and the right hand poses as a reverse palm, simultaneously strike both palms at the lower middle level of the dummy (Po Pai double palm movement). Remember to extend the knees upwards as driving the palms to the dummy, in order to create more power.

13. Utilizing the Biu Ma, slide the right foot round the leg of the dummy and move it back to the center line of the dummy. Simultaneously, drop the right hand into Gaun Sao on the lower arm of the dummy and bring the left hand up into a high Gaun Sao on the outside line of the right arm of the dummy.

14. Shifting to Siu Lim Tao Ma, left hand Huen Sau on right arm of the dummy and right Jum Sau on the left arm of the dummy.

15. Remaining in Siu Lim Tao stance, left hand lower lying palm strike to lower middle part of the right hand outside line of the dummy and right Huen Sau on the left arm of the dummy.

16. Double Jut Sao on outside line of dummy arms.

17. Double Tok Sao on the underside of both upper arms.

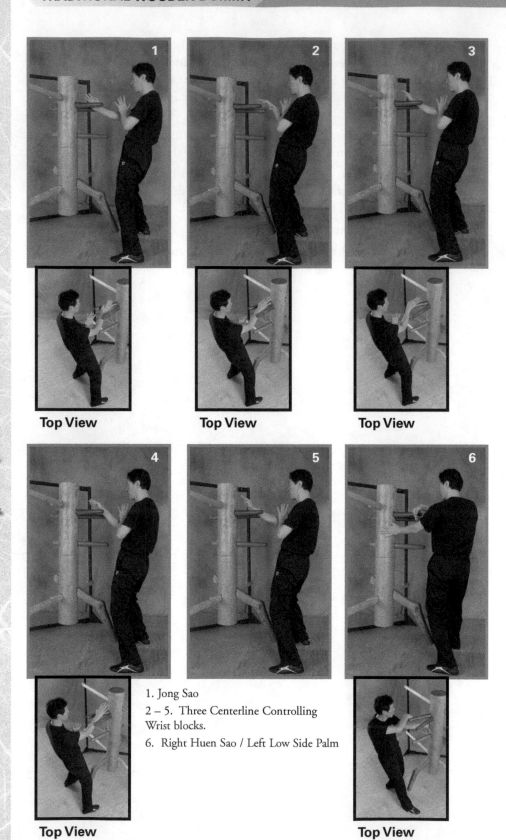

Top View

Top View

Top View

Top View

1. Jong Sao
2 – 5. Three Centerline Controlling Wrist blocks.
6. Right Huen Sao / Left Low Side Palm

Top View

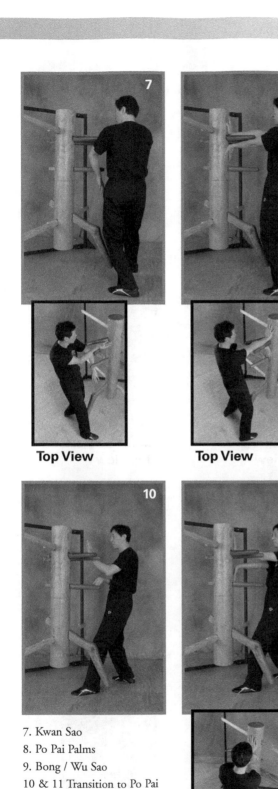

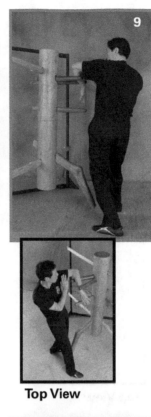

7. Kwan Sao
8. Po Pai Palms
9. Bong / Wu Sao
10 & 11 Transition to Po Pai Palms
12. High / Low Gaun Sao

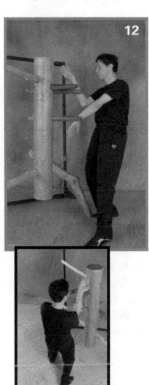

木人樁

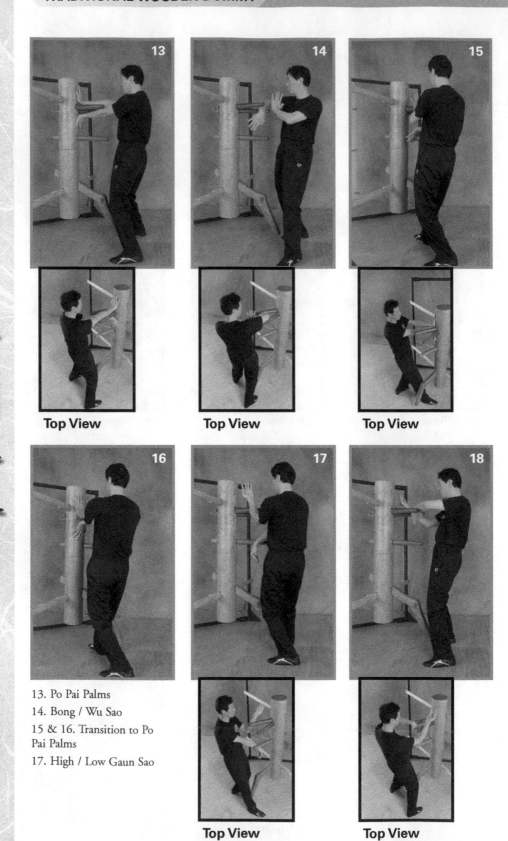

Top View

Top View

Top View

Top View

Top View

13. Po Pai Palms
14. Bong / Wu Sao
15 & 16. Transition to Po Pai Palms
17. High / Low Gaun Sao

Top View

Top View

18. Huen Sao / High Gaun Sao
19. Right Huen Sao / Left Low Side Palm
20. Double Jut Sao
21. Double Tok Sao

Top View

木
人
樁

Introduction to Section Five

Section Five introduces the Faan Sao principle. Faan Sao means "repeating hand" which is exactly the idea. We do not attack with a single hand, but also hit with a 'repeating hand'. Faan Sao is about the idea of continuous attacks. Once the first attack is launched, the Wing Chun fighter should continue to attack without interruption, until the opponent is finished. In the event an attack encounters a blocking hand, the blocking hand is controlled and the next attack launched without delay.

Grandmaster Ip Ching says "Control is the skill of Wing Chun. Hitting the opponent is the goal, but it is control of the opponents bridge (arms) which makes hitting possible." In Section Five of the Wooden Dummy Set, the control of the bridge is emphasized. The Bong Sao / Lop - Fak Sao / Pak – Palm, section teaches the continuous control of the opponent's bridge.

This section also introduces a new kick to the arsenal of the Wing Chun fighter. This crosses stomping kick (Tip Sun Girk) is delivered in a very unique way in this section of the dummy set. The footwork requires the trainee to step around, dynamically shift to face the Dummy (with balance) and deliver the kick from very close range. These skills will build on the foundation already laid by the trainee's earlier Wing Chun training.

Section 5

Face the Dummy in Siu Lim Tao Ma with left hand in Man Sao and left hand in Wu Sao (Jong Sao).

1. Shift to Chum Kiu Ma, transfer the weight to the right leg. Simultaneously, raise the right hand into a high Gaun Sao on the upper left arm of the dummy and drop the left hand up into a low Gaun Sao on the outside line of the lower (left-side) arm of the dummy.

2. Shift to Chum Kiu Ma, transfer the weight to the left leg. Simultaneously, raise the left hand into a high Gaun Sao on the upper right arm of the dummy and drop the right hand up into a low Gaun Sao on the outside line of the lower (right-side) arm of the dummy.

3. Shift to Chum Kiu Ma, transfer the weight to the right leg. Collapse the right arm from your elbow into right Bong Sao on the right arm (inside line) of the dummy (contact area for the block is just above the wrist) and left hand in Wu Sao

4. Shift to Chum Kiu Ma, transfer the weight to the left leg and (simultaneously use "two energy" i.e. pull and strike) change the right hand into a Lop Sao "grappling hand" (ensure the thumb of the grappling hand is at side of arm) and grab the right arm of the dummy and simultaneously with the left hand chopping strike (Fak Sao) at top of dummy.

5. Returning to Siu Lim Tao Ma, left hand Pak Sau on right arm of the dummy and right spade hand strike to upper part of the dummy (left side)

6. Shift to Chum Kiu Ma, transfer the weight to the left leg. Collapse the left arm from your elbow into left Bong Sao on the left arm (inside line) of the dummy (contact area for the block is just above the wrist) and right hand Wu Sao.

7. Shift to Chum Kiu Ma, transfer the weight to the right leg and (simultaneously use "two energy" i.e. pull and strike) change the left hand into a Lop Sao "grappling hand" (ensure the thumb of the grappling hand is at side of arm) and grab the left arm of the dummy and simultaneously with the right hand chopping strike (Fak Sao) at top of dummy (left side).

8. Returning to Siu Lim Tao Ma, right hand Pak Sau on left arm of the dummy and left spade hand strike to upper part of the dummy (right side)

9. Shift to Chum Kiu Ma, transfer the weight to the right leg. Collapse the right arm from your elbow into right Bong Sao on the right arm (inside line) of the dummy (contact area for the block is just above the wrist) and left hand in Wu Sao.

10. Slide the left foot to the left with Biu Ma, slide the right foot towards your left foot and shift to face the dummy in a kicking stance, both feet should be facing the dummy at a 45 degree, then raise the left leg and thrust a crossed stamping kick (Tip Sun Girk) to the right side of the dummy (at height above leg). Simultaneously, keeping the right arm in contact with the right arm of the dummy, roll the right arm under the right arm of the dummy and extend it into Tan Sao on the outside line. Again simultaneously, horizontal palm strike with the left hand to the "ribs" of the dummy.

11. Shift to Chum Kiu Ma, transfer the weight to the left leg. Collapse the left arm from your elbow into left Bong Sao on the left arm (inside line) of the dummy (contact area for the block is just above the wrist) and right hand in Wu Sao.

12. Slide the right foot to the right with Biu Ma, slide the left foot towards your right foot and shift to face the dummy in a kicking stance, both feet should be facing the dummy at a 45 degree, then raise the right leg and thrust a crossed stamping kick (Tip Sun Girk) to the left side of the dummy (at height above leg). Simultaneously, keeping the left arm in contact with the left arm of the dummy, roll the left arm under the left arm of the dummy and extend it into Tan Sao on the outside line. Again, simultaneously, horizontal palm strike with the right hand to the "ribs" of the dummy.

13. Shift to Chum Kiu Ma, transfer the weight to the right leg. Simultaneously, raise the right hand into a high Gaun Sao on the upper left arm of the dummy and drop the left hand up into a low Gaun Sao on the outside line of the lower (left-side) arm of the dummy.

14. Transferring the weight back to the center in Siu Lim Tao Ma, left hand Tok Sau on right arm of the dummy and right Kau Sau on the left arm of the dummy.

15. Remaining in Siu Lim Tao Ma, simultaneously Jut Sao with the left hand on the right hand of the dummy and vertical palm strike the top (face) of the dummy with the right hand Double Jut Sao in a downward direction onto the outside line of dummy.

16. Double Tok Sao on the underside of both arms of the dummy.

葉問詠春

Top View

Top View

Top View

Top View

1. Jong Sao
2. High / Low Gaun Sao
3. High / Low Gaun Sao
4. Bong / Wu Sao
5 & 6. Transition to Lop Sao / Fak Da

Top View

Top View

Top View

7. Pak Sao / Low Straight Punch
8. Bong / Wu Sao
9. Transition to Lop Sao / Fak Da
10. Pak Sao / Side Palm
11. Bong / Wu Sao
12 . Transition to Cross Stamping Kick
with Taun Sao / Plam Strike

Top View

葉問詠春

13 – 14. Transition to Cross Stamping Kick with Taun Sao / Plam Strike

15. Bong / Wu Sao

16 – 18. Transition to Cross Stamping Kick with Taun Sao / Plam Strike

Top View

Top View

Top View

Top View

Top View

Top View

Top View

Top View

19. High / Low Gaun Sao
20. Kau Sao / Tok Sao
21. Jut Sao / High Palm
22. Double Jut Sao
23. Double Tok Sao

木人樁

Introduction to Section Six

Section Six teaches the concept of chain-kicking or linking kicks. Just as Wing Chun utilizes the Lin Wan Kune (Chain Punches), Kicks can be linked into a continuous attacking method as well.

In this Section the trainee will learn the Jek Tek / Tsa Lok Tsuk Girk combination kick. The key principle to chain kicking is that of kicking from a balanced base, and not leaning into the kick, and depending on making contact with the kick to keep your balance. Prior to kicking the trainee will have to shift from Siu Lim Tao Ma into the kicking position which has the heels shifting together from the original position.

The next skill covered in this Section is that of the coordination of the step / Pak Sao / Dai Jeung in order to hit with structure and power. This skill brings together the concept known as the trinity of motion (body + step + hand). This concept must be mastered in order to apply Kung Fu in a real fight; otherwise you will lack authority in your techniques.

Section 6

Face the Dummy in Siu Lim Tao Ma with left hand in Man Sao and left hand in Wu Sao.

1. Remaining in Siu Lim Tao Ma, simultaneously place hands in guard position and forward left Tan Sao towards the right arm (inside line) of the dummy (right hand in Wu Sao), transfer the weight onto the left leg and kick with a right leg Front Kick((Jek Tek) towards the left middle section of the dummy (above the leg).

2. Keep the weight on the left leg (turning the body 45 degrees to the right side of the dummy) and kick a right Downward Side Kick (Tsa Lok Tsuk Geuk) to the leg of the dummy, right hand in Bong Sao and left in Wu Sao position.

3. Returning to Siu Lim Tao Ma, simultaneously place hands in guard position and forward right hand Tan Sao towards the left arm (inside line) of the dummy (left hand in Wu Sao), transfer the weight onto the right leg and kick with a left leg Front Kick (Jek Tek) towards the right middle section of the dummy (above the leg).

4. Keep the weight on the right leg (turning the body 45 degrees to the left side of the dummy) and kick a left Downward Side Kick (Tsa Lok Tsuk Geuk) to the leg of the dummy, left hand in Bong Sao and right in Wu Sao position.

5. Returning to Siu Lim Tao Ma, then shift to the left to Chum Kiu Ma, with the weight on the right leg and with the right hand Pak Sau on the lower arm of the dummy (left hand in Wu Sao).

6. Slide the left foot to the left and, utilizing Sip Ma slide the right foot round the leg of the dummy and move forward with energy into contact with the leg of the dummy. Note the left foot pivots to face the dummy and the right foot is parallel to the left. Simultaneously, left Pak Sau on the right arm of the dummy (outside line) and right lower lying palm strike to the left side of the dummy (at mid lower level/ribs level).

7. Returning to Chum Kiu Ma slide to the right with both feet but have the weight on your back left leg, and using your left hand Gum Sau (Pak Sau) on the lower arm of the dummy (right hand in Wu Sao).

8. Slide the right foot to the right and, utilizing Sip Ma, slide the left foot round the leg of the dummy and move it into contact with the leg of the dummy. Note the right foot pivots to face the dummy and the left foot is parallel to the right. Simultaneously, right Pak Sau on the left arm of the dummy (outside line) and left lower lying palm strike to the right side of the dummy (at mid lower level/ribs level).

9. Stepping back out with the left foot to Chum Kiu Ma, transfer the weight to the right leg. Simultaneously, raise the right hand into a high Gaun Sao on the upper left arm of the dummy and drop the left hand up into a low Gaun Sao on the outside line of the lower (left-side) arm of the dummy.

10. Transferring the weight back to the center in Siu Lim Tao Ma, left hand jum sau on right arm of the dummy and right Huen Sau on the left arm of the dummy.

11. Remaining in Siu Lim Tao Ma, simultaneously jut sao with the left hand on the right hand of the dummy and vertical palm strike the face of the dummy with the right hand.

12. Double Jut Sao in a downward direction onto the outside line of dummy arms.

13. Double Tok Sao underneath dummy arms.

1. Jong Sao

2. Left Taun / Wu Sao with Right Front Kick

3. Bong / Wu Sao with Downward Side Kick

4. Jong Sao

5. Right Taun / Wu Sao with Left Front Kick

6. Bong / Wu Sao with Downward Side Kick

Top View

Top View

Top View

Top View

木人樁

89

Top View

7 & 8. Transition to Pak / Wu Sao

9 & 10. Transition to Pak Sao / Side Palm

11. Pak / Wu Sao

12 & 13. Transition to Pak Sao / Side Palm

Top View

Top View

14. High / Low Gaun Sao

15. Jum Sao / Huen Sao

16. Left Jut Sao / Right Straight Palm

17. Double Jut Sao

18. Double Tok Sao

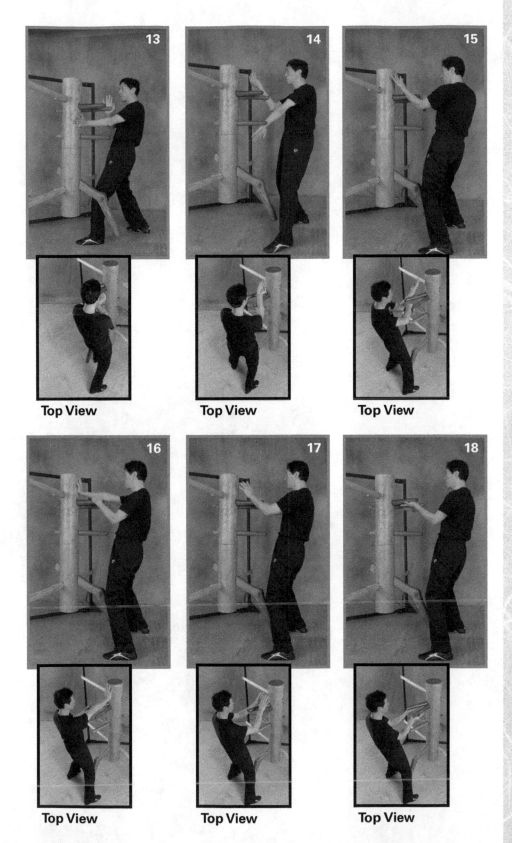

Top View

Top View

Top View

Top View

Top View

Top View

木人樁

91

Introduction to Section Seven

Section Seven begins with the Dai Bong Sao / Taun Sao / Wang Jern combination. Then stepping outside, passing the punch thrown by the dummy followed by the application of the stomp kick (Tek Girk) to the Dummy's Knee.

This section also introduces the Sew Girk (Sweep Kick). This is a kick that is not seen in the three hand forms leading up to the Dummy Set. The Sew Girk is applied in combination with the control of the opponent's arm, which in actual application can be either a pulling control or a jamming control.

This is the last section of the traditional dummy form taught by Grandmaster Ip Man. While there are other ways to count the sections, resulting in some confusion as to whether there are seven, eight, nine or sometimes as many as thirteen sections of the Dummy Form, we believe the best reference as to Ip Man's Wing Chun Dummy Form was left by the grandmaster himself, on 8mm film, just days prior to his death. Out of respect to the late Grandmaster, we attempt to keep the form as he demonstrated it.

Section 7 – Final Section

1. Utilizing the shifting Chum Kiu Ma, transfer the weight to the right leg, collapse the right arm from your elbow into right Bong Sao on the lower arm (inside line) of the dummy (contact area for the block is just above the wrist), left hand Wu Sao.

2. Utilizing the shifting Chum Kiu Ma, transfer the weight to the left leg, collapse the left arm from your elbow into left Bong Sao on the lower arm (inside line) of the dummy (contact area for the block is just above the wrist), right hand Wu Sao.

3. Utilizing the shifting Chum Kiu Ma, transfer the weight to the right leg, collapse the right arm from your elbow into right Bong Sao on the lower arm (inside line) of the dummy (contact area for the block is just above the wrist), left hand Wu Sao.

4. Returning to Siu Lim Tao Ma, raise the right hand into Tan Sau position on the left arm of the dummy (inside line), left hand in Wu Sao.

5. Remaining in Siu Lim Tao Ma, raise the right hand into upper lying palm (spade) position on the top of the dummy (left side), left hand in Wu Sao.

6. Slide to the left (past the right arm of the dummy) shift and face the dummy Simultaneously, right hand in wu sau position, and the left arm up to Pak Sao on the outside line of the right arm of the dummy and kick with an 'off-body' lower thrust kick (Tek) with your right leg to the leg of the dummy. Note the left foot pivots to face the dummy and the left foot is parallel to the right, your weight is on the left leg.

7. Utilizing the shifting Chum Kiu Ma, transfer the weight to the left leg, collapse the left arm from your elbow into left Bong Sao on the lower arm (inside line) of the dummy (contact area for the block is just above the wrist), right hand Wu Sao.

8. Utilizing the shifting Chum Kiu Ma, transfer the weight to the right leg, collapse the right arm from your elbow into right Bong Sao on the lower arm (inside line) of the dummy (contact area for the block is just above the wrist), left hand Wu Sao.

9. Utilizing the shifting Chum Kiu Ma, transfer the weight to the left leg, collapse the left arm from your elbow into left Bong Sao on the lower arm (inside line) of the dummy (contact area for the block is just above the wrist), right hand Wu Sao.

10. Returning to Siu Lim Tao stance, raise the left hand into Tan Sau position on the right arm of the dummy (inside line), right hand in Wu Sao.

11. Remaining in Siu LimTao stance, raise the left hand into upper lying palm (spade) position on the top of the dummy (right side), right hand in Wu Sao.

12. Slide to the right (past the left arm of the dummy) shift and face the dummy Simultaneously, left hand in wu sau position, and the right arm up to Pak Sao on the outside line of the left arm of the dummy, and kick with an 'off body' lower thrust kick (Tek) with your left leg to the leg of the dummy. Note the right foot pivots to face the dummy and the right foot is parallel to the left, your weight is on the right leg.

13. Utilizing the turn from Chum Kiu, transfer the weight to the right leg. Collapse the right arm from your elbow into right Bong Sao on the right arm (inside line) of the dummy (contact area for the block is just above the wrist) and left hand Wu Sao.

14. Slide the left foot slightly to the left and, shift to face the dummy, both feet should be facing the dummy at a 45 degree angle, then raise the right leg and launch a sweeping kick (Sew Geuk) to the leg of the dummy – simultaneously - change the right Bong Sau arm to a grapping hand on the right arm of the dummy (on the outside line) and grab (Lop Sao) with the left hand on the same arm of the dummy.

    You should utilize a pulling motion towards you with your hands as you are launching the kick.

15. Utilizing the shifting Chum Kiu Ma, transfer the weight to the left leg. Collapse the left arm from your elbow into left Bong Sao on the left arm (inside line) of the dummy (contact area for the block is just above the wrist) and right hand Wu Sao.

16. Slide the right foot slightly to the right and, shift to face the dummy, both feet should be facing the dummy at a 45 degree angle, then raise the left leg and launch a sweeping kick (Sew Geuk) to the leg of the dummy – simultaneously - change the left Bong Sau arm to a grapping hand on the left arm of the dummy (on the outside line) and grab (Lop Sao) with the right hand on the same arm of the dummy.

    You should utilize a pulling motion towards you with your hands as you are launching the kick.

17. Utilizing the shifting Chum Kiu Ma, transfer the weight to the right leg. Simultaneously, raise the right hand into a high Gaun Sao on the upper left arm of the dummy and drop the left hand up into a low Gaun Sao on the outside line of the lower (left-side) arm of the dummy.

18. Transferring the weight back to the center in Siu Lim Tao Ma, left hand Jum (Gaun) sau on right arm of the dummy and right Huen Sau on the left arm of the dummy.

19. Remaining in Siu Lim Tao Ma, simultaneously jut sao with the left hand on the right hand of the dummy and vertical palm strike the face of the dummy with the right hand.

20. Remaining in Siu Lim Tao Ma, simultaneously double Jut Sau on both the upper arms of the dummy on the outside line.

21. Remaining in Siu Lim Tao Ma, simultaneously double Tok Sau on both the upper arms of the dummy.

葉問詠春

1. Jong Sao
2. Low Bong / Wu Sao
3. Low Bong / Wu Sao
4. Low Bong / Wu Sao
5. Right Taun / Wu Sao
6. Right Side Palm / Wu Sao

Top View

Top View

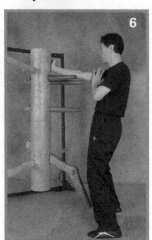

Top View

Top View

Top View

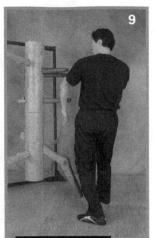

7 & 8. Transition to Pak / Wu Sao with Off Body Low Thrust Kick to Knee

9. Low Bong / Wu Sao

10. Low Bong / Wu Sao

11. Low Bong / Wu Sao

12 . Left Taun / Wu Sao

Top View

Top View

Top View

Top View

Top View

13

14

15

Top View

13. Left Side Palm / Wu Sao

14 & 15. Transition to Pak / Wu Sao with Off Body Low Thrust Kick to Knee

16. Bong / Wu Sao

17 & 18. Transition to Lop Sao Arm Control with Sweeping Kick

Top View

16

17

18

Top View

Top View

Top View

19. Bong / Wu Sao
20 – 22. Transition to Lop Sao Arm
Control with Sweeping Kick
23. High / Low Gaun Sao
24. High Gaun Sao / Huen Sao

木人樁

Top View   **Top View**   **Top View**

Top View

Top View

25. Left Jut Sao / Right High Palm
26. Double Jut Sao
27. Double Tok Sao
28. Finish

Top View

1. Tony Massengill faces Samuel Kwok

2. Massengill launches a right jab, Kwok intercepts the jab with a Mon Sao

3. Kwok applies a Lop Sao and palm strike.

Massengill slips the palm, at which time Kwok converts the palm into a neck control.

4. Kwok applies a neck pull and simultaneous punch to Massengill's face.

1. Massengill and Kwok square off

2. Massengill attacks with a right jab, which Kwok intercepts with a right side Bong Sao

3. As Massengill's Jab is deflected, Kwok fol-lows the deflection by passing the hand with a Taun Sao / Palm Strike to the ribs.

4. Followed by a left hand Pak Sao / Punch to Massengill's head.

木人樁

1. Massengill and Kwok square off.

2. Massengill launches a right jab which Kwok deflects with a scissors Gaun Sao

3. Massengill throws a cross, which Kwok deflects by applying Kwan Sao.

4. Massengill throws a right hook which is stopped by Kwok's Taun Sao / Palm.

1. Massengill and Kwok square off.

2. Massengill launches a right jab which Kwok deflects with a left Pak Sao.

3. Massengill throws a cross, which Kwok deflects by applying a crossing Pak Sao.

4. Kwok follows the Pak Sao with a Fak Da attack to Massengill's throat.

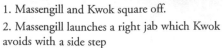

1. Massengill and Kwok square off.

2. Massengill launches a right jab which Kwok avoids with a side step

3. Simultaneously applying a Pak / Fak Sao to deflect the punch .

4. Kwok finishes the altercation with a Side Kick / Bong Sao Cover.

1. Master Kwok and Stephen Rigby square off with one another.

2. Kwok closes and creates bridge contact with both of Rigby's hands.

3 & 4. Kwok utilizes a double Huen Sao to

control Rigby's hands and gain access in order to do a double palm strike to the ribs.

5. Rigby runs his hands to attack Kwok's face. Kwok defends with a double Taun Sao.

6. Kwok strikes with a double palm strike to Rigby's face.

7. Rigby runs the hands to attack Kwok's body. Kwok guards with a double Jaum Sao.

8 – 10. Kwok uses a left Huen Sao to open for a palm strike to the ribs and follows with a double palm to Rigby's face.

(Note: Generally when a double movement is utilized in either the empty hand forms or the Mook Jong, it is for symmetry, not fighting application.)

1. Massengill and Kwok square off.

2. Kwok side-steps

3. Kwok defends with a Taun Sao and simultaneous kick to the knee of Massengill's front leg.

4. Kwok follows with an elbow attack to Massengill's eye.

1. Massengill and Kwok square off.

2. Massengill launches the Jab as part of a Jab / Cross combination. Kwok counters with a Inside wrist flick.

3. As Massengill launches the Cross punch, Kwok intercepts the line with a Biu Sao and simultaneous punch.

1. Massengill and Kwok square off.

2. Massengill attacks with a right Jab.

3. Kwok intercepts with a right cutting hand which transitions upon contact to a Huen Sao to open the outside line for attack.

4. Kwok attacks with a low lying palm.

5. & 6. Kwok follows up with a Po Pai (Double Palm).

1. Massengill and Kwok square off.

2. Massengill attacks with a Jab. Kwok defends with Pak Sao.

3. Massengill launches a Cross. Kwok intercepts with Taun Sao

4. & 5. Kwok closes in on Massengill and attacks with Po Pai Palms.

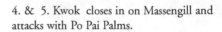

1. Rigby and Kwok square off.

2. Rigby attacks with a Jab. Kwok defends with a Bong Sao which passes the punch.

3. Kwok counters with a Lop Sao and Fak Da attack.

4. Rigby attacks with a Cross. Kwok defends with a receiving Pak Sao and straight punch.

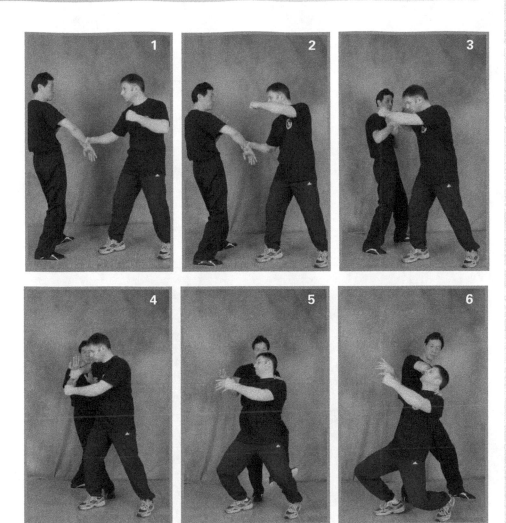

1. Rigby grabs Kwok's arm to control and launch a punch.

2. Rigby throws the punch.

3. Kwok sidesteps,

4. And utilizes the crossing step to gain access to Rigby's back.

5. Kwok attacks Rigby's leg from behind with a kick to the back of the knee.

6. Kwok finishes with an elbow attack to Rigby's face, while controlling his body.

1. Massengill and Kwok square off.

2. Massengill attacks with a Jab. Kwok intercepts with Jong Sao and a Kick to the hip area.

3. Controlling Massengill's arm,

4. Kwok follows with a Side kick to Massengill's knee,

5. And finishes with a punch to the head.

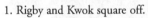

1. Rigby and Kwok square off.

2. Rigby attacks with a Jab. Kwok defends with Bong Sao while stepping to the outside.

3. Kwok applies a Lop Sao and arm break.

4 – 6. Then he applies a Sew Girk kick to the shin.

1. Massengill attacks with a Side Kick

2 – 4. Kwok sidesteps and applies a Gaun Sao and Side Kick to Massengill's supporting leg.

1. Massengill and Kwok square off.

2 & 3. Massengill attacks with a Front Kick. Kwok sidesteps and applies an outside Gum Sao,

4. Utilizing Biu Ma, Kwok attacks with a punch while controlling Massengill's front arm.

1. Massengill attacks with a low Jab.

2. Kwok shifts and applies a low Bong Sao.

3. Massengill follows with a right Cross.

4. Kwok sidesteps and applies a Pak/Wu Sao defense with a simultaneous Stomp Kick to the inside knee of Massengill's supporting leg.

1. Massengill and Kwok square off.

2. Kwok attacks with a straight punch. Massengill defends with an outside stepping Bong Sao.

3. Massengill applies a Lop Sao arm control.

4. Massengill attacks with a straight punch.

5 - 7. Kwok defeats the attack with a Pak / Fak Sao defense with a Biu Ma advancing step.

木人椿

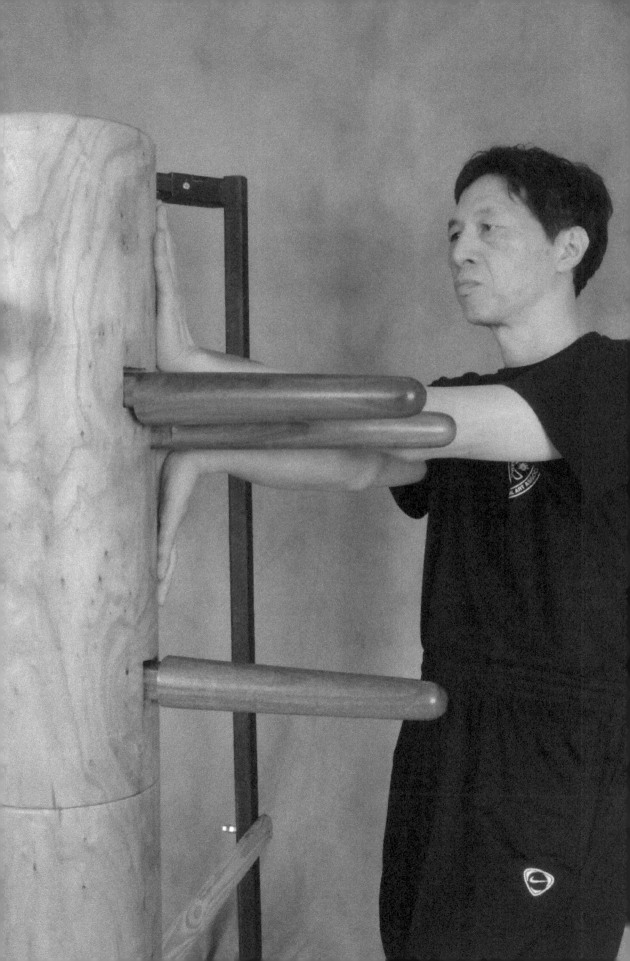

Glossary

Techniques in Chinese Alphabetical Order

Biu Sao

The Biu Sao or thrusting fingers is one of the many Wing Chun moves which can be used both as a block and as a strike. It can be used to strike or block anything around shoulder height or above. Or it can be used to strike to the eyes and throat.

Bong Sao

The Bong Sao or wing arm is quite a complex Wing Chun movement that features largely in the system's forms.

Fak Sao

The Fak Sao is a chop that first learnt from Sil Lim Tao Wing Chun's first form. A good move to use when the practitioner is unsure of what is coming, this move is similar but not the same as the Man Sao.

Fook Sao

The Fook Sao or bridge-on arm is relatively simple but effective Wing Chun movement that features largely in the system's first form. It is primarily used in Chi Sao but can be applied as a block.

Gaun Sao (low)

The low Gaun Sao or Splitting block is used to block attacks to the mid section. It is an essential part of the Wing Chun blocking arsenal.

Gaun Sao (high)

The high Gaun Sao or Splitting block is slightly more complex block than its lower counterpart, hence it is found in the third form and not the first. But when both Gaun Sao's are performed together they can cover and block almost any attack on the body.

Gum Sao

The Gum Sao or pinning hand is found in the first form and is used as a block or to pin an opponents arm (hence its name), It is often used in Chi Sao.

Huen Sao

The Huen Sao or circling hand is an essential Wing Chun technique found throughout the system's 3 hand forms. It can be performed clockwise or counter-clockwise depending on the situations need.

Ju Cheung

Ju Cheung is a powerful "sideward palm" strike that uses the heel of the palm to strike an opponent.

Jum Sao

The Jum Sao is yet another technique which can be used both as a block and a strike however, it is one of the few Wing Chun blocks which is performed with power, that is not to say the block uses a clash of force just that power is applied to 'strike' when blocking to cause damage the aggressor.

Jut Sao

The Jut Sao or sinking hand is an extremely effective block which can throw the balance of the opponent whilst leaving the practitioners hand in the perfect place for a counter strike.

Kop Sao

The Kop Sao or downward hand is a movement found in the second form Chun Kiu. The Kop Sao is not strictly a technique in its own right it is a blend of Gum Sao, Pak Sao and Jut Sao. The Kop Sao can be applied practically and it is also used in Chi Sao.

Kop Jarn

Kop Jarn is a downward elbow motion which is repeatedly performed in the 3rd form and can be used both as a block or a powerful close range strike.

Kwan Sao

Kwan Sao is a relatively complex rotating arm motion which can be used to block or roll out of a trap and is found in the dummy form.

Lan Sao

The Lan Sao or bar arm, is a lifting block. It looks similar to the Bong Sao but unlike the Bong Sao the arm forearm is level with the shoulders and more or less parallel to the body and the rotation in the forearm is up not across.

Lap Sao

The Lap Sao is an interesting technique that destroys the balance and structure of an opponent, it has many uses most of which will be accompanied by a strike to deliver devastating force.

Lin Wan Kuen

Lim Wan Kuen or chain punching describes the rapid delivery of straight punches from the centerline.

Man Sao

Man Sao or inquisitive arm is used to gain contact with the opponent and can be used to block in a variety of ways.

Pak Sao

The Pak Sao or Slap Block is a simple yet effective block which is like many Wing Chun moves is the adaptation and refinement of a natural reflex to being attacked.

Pie Jarn

Pie Jarn is a horizontal hacking elbow strike that can be performed turning towards the target or away from the target. The power for it is developed in Chun Kiu

Po Pai Cheung

Po Pai is a complex double palm motion found in the Dummy form of the Wing Chun system, it can be used to strike, push or aggressively advance whilst maintaining positioning in the center line.

Taun Sao

Taun Sao is an essential, common and yet effective Wing Chun block, this is found largely in the first form and dummy form.

Tok Sao

Tok Sao or lifting hand can be used to lift an opponents guard at the elbow in order to strike them or to throw them off balance.

Wu Sao

The Wu Sao or guard hand should always remain up when a hand is not in use as an extra failsafe cover. The Wu Sao should be in the perfect position to be launched forward as a block or strike.

NOTES

NOTES

MASTERING WING CHUN
The Keys To Ip Man's Kung Fu (DVD Series)
by Grandmaster Samuel Kwok

VOL. 1 - SIU LIM TAO (LITTLE IDEA)

Siu Lim Tao is the firsthand form of the Wing Chun Kung Fu system. The form teaches the correct hand and arm positions for attack and defense. Development and use of energy are the focus of Siu Lim Tao training. In this informative DVD, Grandmaster Samuel Kwok teaches the correct method of performing the form as handed down by Ip Man, and gives the student the keys to training the foundation of the Ip Man Wing Chun Kung Fu method. Instruction includes the correct method of performing the form, as well as training methods and the application of each technique.

#302 - $24.95 - ISBN-13: 978-1-934347-16-4

VOL. 2 - CHUM KIU (SEEKING THE BRIDGE)

Chum Kiu is the second form in the Wing Chun Kung Fu system. This form teaches the dynamic application of the techniques learned in Wing Chun's first form Siu Lim Tao. While the first form teaches the correct structure of the attacks and defensive movements, it is in Chum Kiu that the student learns to "seek the bridge" and use both hands simultaneously, such as one hand defending while the other attacks. Chum Kiu teaches stepping and footwork, and also Wing Chun's specialized kicking method and the generation of power through the correct method of using the entire body in stance turning (Yiu Ma). In this DVD, Grandmaster Kwok also demonstrates and explains in detail the use of Wing Chun's devastating short-range power.

#303 - $24.95 - ISBN-13: 978-1-934347-17-1

VOL. 3 - BIU GEE (THRUSTING FINGERS)

Biu Gee "thrusting fingers," also known as "first aid hand," is the last hand form taught in the Ip Man Wing Chun system. Biu Gee training is one of the keys to learning to focus energy into a strike. Biu Gee also develops devastating striking power by combining focused strikes with the rotational energy developed by correct stance turning (Yiu Ma), as learned in the previous training of the Chum Kiu form. Another key of Biu Gee training is to train the hands to regain the center if the centerline is lost or unguarded. The Biu Gee form teaches two unique methods of footwork, the use of "Two Direction Energy" and how to control the opponent and effectively use continuous striking movements. In this DVD, Grandmaster Kwok demonstrates the proper method of training this devastating form.

#304 - $24.95 - ISBN-13: 978-1-934347-18-8

Vol. 4 – CHI SAO

This is a unique and refreshing insight into the Chi Sao element of Ip Man's original Wing Chun Kung Fu. In this DVD, all the major drills and trapping theories are investigated with explosive applications. You will learn the techniques of Chi Sao: basic hand techniques, single hand and double hand drills, and footwork, correct body structure alignment, body turning, etc…

Chi Sao constitutes the most important training method in the Wing Chun system. It is what Ip Man referred to as the Genius of Wing Chun.

Training in Chi Sao will help you develop contact reflexes, which is the key to victory in a live combat situation. Chi Sao training develops close quarter coordination and close quarter focus; improves mobility, balance, timing, and accuracy, and creates ample targets and openings in which to attack and counter. This DVD is demonstrated by Grandmaster Samuel Kwok, one of the world's most respected Ip Man Wing Chun Kung Fu technicians.

#336 – US$24.95 - ISBN: 978-1-934347-98-0

Vol. 5 – WOODEN DUMMY

The Wing Chun wooden training dummy is a training device designed to correct technique and structure as well as increase power, speed, accuracy, and conditioning.

You'll learn the true Original Ip Man's Wing Chun Wooden Dummy form from Grandmaster Samuel Kwok. This DVD is a complete step-by-step guide to the Wooden Dummy hands techniques, legs application, and footwork. All the original sections are demonstrated clearly from start to finish, in different camera angles to facilitate easy and accurate learning. There also is a general commentary and description of each segment and its most common training mistakes to improve not only your technique, but your level of understanding. In addition to teaching the skills on the Wooden Dummy, Grandmaster Samuel Kwok demonstrates the applications of the Wooden Dummy training techniques on a partner, giving you an excellent idea of the combat effectiveness of each movement.

#337 – US$24.95 - ISBN: 978-1-934347-99-7

Order at: www.em3video.com

MASTERING WING CHUN

By Samuel Kwok & Tony Massengill

In this book, the keys to the Ip Man Wing Chun Kung Fu system are explained. The three hand sets are shown in detail, along with the application of the key movements. One of the keys to Wing Chun is laying a proper foundation. The first form Siu Lim Tao (Little Idea) is the development of that foundation. While the first form teaches the correct structure of the attacks and defensive movements, it is in Chum Kiu that the student learns to "seek the bridge" and use both hands simultaneously, such as one hand defending while the other attacks. The third form, Biu Gee (Thrusting Fingers), also known as the (First Aid) form, teaches the keys to recovery from the loss of a superior position in fighting. Biu Gee training is one of the keys to learning to focus energy into a strike. Also covered is the Chi Sao (Sticking Hands) training of Wing Chun, as well as the key principles that have made Ip Man Wing Chun one of the most famous Kung Fu systems in the world.

#313 – US $24.95 – 7 X 10 – 304 pages – ISBN: 978-1-933901-26-8

Order at: www.empirebooks.net

Please visit us at
www.kwokwingchun.com
www.ipmanwingchun.com

www.EfficientWarrior.com

CPSIA information can be obtained
at www.ICGtesting.com
Printed in the USA
LVHW09s2342090818
586464LV00010B/28/P